SCROOGE'S GUIDE TO CHRISTMAS

SCROOGE'S GUIDE TO CHRISTMAS
BY RICHARD WILSON & DAVID ROPER

Hodder & Stoughton

First published in Great Britain in 1997
by Hodder and Stoughton
A division of Hodder Headline PLC

British Library Cataloguing in Publication Data

Wilson, Richard
Scrooge's Guide to Christmas
1. English wit and humour 2. Christmas - Humour
I. Title
828 . 9 ' 14 ' 02

ISBN 0 340 70747 X

Designed by Design/Section
Photographs by Colin Thomas
Stylist Glynis Cox
Make-up Karen ZM Turner
Assistant Robert Smith

ACKNOWLEDGEMENTS

Matthew Thompson

Nick Barre
Charlotte Barton
Rupert Lancaster
David Lewis
Malik Meer
Deborah Owen
Colin Paterson
Delia Smith

The author and publishers are grateful to the following
copyright holders for permission to quote copyright material:
A Christmas Carol © 1954 Tom Lehrer, p.19 The Society of Authors on behalf of the Bernard Shaw
Estate: from *An Atrocious Institution* by George Bernard Shaw, p.38; Jennifer Gosse: from *Father & Son*
by Edmund Gosse, p.54; MacMillan London Ltd: from *Take it Like a Man* by George O'Dowd, p.76; Warner
Chappell Music: from *The Twelve Days of Christmas* by Allen Sherman, p.89; Century: from *Craig Brown's
Greatest Hits* by Craig Brown, p.93; Kris Publishing/Elmo Publishing/Universal Songs administered
by CopyCare: from *Grandma Got Run Over by a Reindeer* by Randy Brooks, p.101; Faber and Faber Ltd: from
A Christmas Poem by Wendy Cope, p.119

Every reasonable effort has been made to acknowledge the ownership of the copyrighted material included
in this volume. Any errors that may have occurred are inadvertent, and will be corrected in subsequent
editions provided notification is sent to the publisher.

Photograph on Pp.12-13 reproduced by courtesy of the Scott Polar Research Institute, Cambridge.

Printed and bound in Italy

Hodder and Stoughton
A division of Hodder Headline PLC
338 Euston Road
London NW1 3BH

For Susie Belbin and David Renwick

CONTENTS

FOREWORD

You won't believe this, but my family has been carrying around a dark and shameful burden for the last century and a half. A secret that almost ruined the Clan, forcing my great-great-grandfather to change our historic surname to the common and rather anonymous Wilson. And all because our ancestor, one of the most respected gentlemen in all Britain, whose description appears on the next pages, sold out. Betraying millennia of firmly held beliefs and stout prejudices, he weakened in the face of the Spirit of Christmas.

But now, I am finally able to 'come out' and wash this nasty stain from our bloodline. The truth is, my great-great-great-grandpappy was Ebenezer Scrooge, he of fist so tight that his fingernails pierced his palms. This admirable miser

suddenly turned soft and shamed us all. Yes, I am today proud to admit that I was baptised Richard Ebenezer Scrooge, to remind me never to stray from the path of Humbug and to guard for ever against Tiny Tims who might limp their way into my stony-cold heart.

Christmas, for many of us, is that time of year when people get all emotional over their family ties – especially if they have to wear them. And that's Christmas, really. A time when we exchange lots of things we'd like to keep for lots of things we don't want. A time when your bank balance is seasonally adjusted to take into account the fact that you're about to buy this year's presents with next year's money.

So here it is. The guide to staying sane throughout the Christmas and January sales period. A pocket-book that helps you to take precautions, with detailed advice on how to avoid the season of goodwill altogether … and still live happily ever after.

And who better to embrace this new philosophy than old Scrooge himself – a man who revels in the meanness that Christmas brings out in so many people. And what is Scroogeness, now that we are all to rediscover it before the millennium crashes into us with a jolt? Scroogeness could be defined as a thin layer of rage masking a desire to expose and name Humbug in all its forms. Scrooge is the sceptic who dares to call tinsel tacky, the realist who eschews sentimentality. Scrooge dares to drill down deeper than the reindeer manure, down into his past hurts and heartaches caused by the so-called festive season, down to the deepest gnarled roots that tap into his tortured soul. No, he does not like Christmess.

Long live the Scrooge within us, for deep within this Scrooge is the innocent heart from which shimmers a true light to expose the false merriment and sham celebrations. And, if you don't yet believe me, just turn the page and remind yourself of my dearly beloved ancestor, as described by Charles Dickens himself.

Like Scrooge in Dickens's book, I urge you to follow the message of hope in this book. Read it carefully, and it will enable you to spend less, to entertain with complete disregard for the comfort of your guests (especially your family!) and generally help you to feel good about presenting a dour, mean face to the world between mid-November and the end of January every year for the rest of your life …

A CHRISTMAS CAROL

by Charles Dickens

Oh! But he was a tight-fisted hand at the grindstone, Scrooge! A squeezing, wrenching, grasping, scraping, clutching, covetous old sinner! Hard and sharp as flint, from which no steel had ever struck out generous fire; secret, and self-contained, and solitary as an oyster. The cold within him froze his old features, nipped his pointed nose, shrivelled his cheek, stiffened his gait; made his eyes red, his thin lips blue; and spoke out shrewdly in his grating voice. A frosty rime was on his head, and on his eyebrows, and his wiry chin. He carried his own low temperature always about with him; he iced his office in the dog-days; and didn't thaw it one degree at Christmas.

External heat and cold had little influence on Scrooge. No warmth could warm, nor wintry weather chill him. No wind that blew was bitterer than he, no falling snow was more intent upon its purpose, no pelting rain less open to entreaty. Foul weather didn't know where to have him. The heaviest rain, and snow, and hail, and sleet could boast of the advantage over him in only one respect. They often 'came down' handsomely, and Scrooge never did.

Nobody ever stopped him on the street to say, with gladsome looks, 'My dear Scrooge, how are you? When will you come to see me?' No beggars implored him to bestow a trifle, no children asked him what it was o'clock, no man or woman ever once in all his life inquired the way to such and such a place, of Scrooge. Even the blindmen's dogs appeared to know him; and when they saw him coming on, would tug their owners into doorways and up courts; and then would wag their tails as though they said, 'no eye at all is better than an evil eye, dark master!'

But what did Scrooge care? It was the very thing he liked. To edge his way along the crowded paths of life, warning all human sympathy to keep its distance, was what the knowing ones call 'nuts' to Scrooge.

Once upon a time – of all the good days in the year, on Christmas Eve – old Scrooge sat busy in his counting-house.

'A merry Christmas, uncle! God save you!' cried a cheerful voice. It was the voice of Scrooge's nephew, who came upon him so quickly that this was the first intimation he had of his approach.

'Bah!' said Scrooge. 'Humbug.

'Merry Christmas! Out upon merry Christmas! What's Christmas time to you but a time for paying bills without money; a time for finding yourself a year older, and not an hour richer; a time for balancing your books and having every item in 'em through a round dozen months presented dead against you? If I could work my will,' said Scrooge, indignantly, 'every idiot who goes about with "Merry Christmas" on his lips should be boiled with his own pudding and buried with a stake of holly through his heart. He should!'

A Brief History of Bad Christmases Past

You could say it all went horribly wrong when King Herod didn't quite finish the job, but whatever or whoever ultimately takes the blame, we are not the first, nor will we be the last, to have to live through the horror of Christmas. And, having done so last year, it's worth bearing in mind that there's another one due in less than twelve months.

Matters were almost put right in 692 when the Trullan Council condemned the baking of cakes in honour of the Virgin's 'afterbirth'.

Following this, we have to wait until Oliver Cromwell and his Commonwealth take up cudgels against Yuletide in 1654, when the Prayer Book Service for Christmas was abolished, together with a ban on puddings and mince-pies, as the following verse testifies:

The high-shoe lords of Cromwell's making
were not for dainties – roasting baking:
The chiefest food they found most good in
was rusty bacon and bag-pudding;
Plum-broth was popish, and mince-pie –
O that was flat idolatry.

Little over a decade later, in 1666, Mrs Samuel Pepys was putting the Great Fire of London behind her, and pressing out her mince-pies, or rather overseeing her maids doing so until four in the morning. Understandably, she felt like a lie-in the following morning, while her diarist husband went off to church alone. In the afternoon, still alone, he walked off towards the Temple to see a play, but could not find a theatre open. So what did he do next? Made for home, where until eight o'clock he busied himself putting the titles of his books in alphabetical order.

On Christmas Day 1794, Parson James Woodforde was somewhat under the weather, having had an epileptic fit in the morning, so for lunch he had just 'Sirloin of Beef rosted and plenty of plumb Pudding for dinner & strong beer after'. By Boxing Day he was a little chirpier, and after a more copious repast proceeded to '7, or 8 glasses of Port Wine, which seemed to do me much good'.

A sprig of artificial holly, little more than a twig with a wire stem, green cloth for foliage and cotton wool balls lacquered red for berries, was enough to raise the morale of Captain Scott and Sir Ernest Shackleton as they endured starvation and exhaustion on an unsuccessful attempt to reach the South Pole. It was conjured up unexpectedly on Christmas Day 1902.

I had observed Shackleton ferreting about in his bundle, out of which he presently produced a spare sock. Stored away in that sock was a small round object about the size of a cricket ball, which when brought to light, proved to be a noble plum pudding. Another dive into his lucky-bag and out came a crumpled piece of artificial holly. Heated in the cocoa, our plum pudding was soon steaming hot, and stood on the cooker-lid crowned with its decoration. Our Christmas Day had proved a delightful break in an otherwise uninterrupted spell of semi-starvation. Some days elapsed before its pleasing effects wore off.

Whatever it may be to adults, Christmas remains something very special for the young ones in our lives, though they often have to put on a brave face when they're finally allowed out of bed on that most exciting of mornings, only to discover, as they unwrap gift after gift, that Santa didn't get it quite right. Sometimes they manage to put a terrifically brave face on things … though children like the young Truman Capote are more likely to give voice to their feelings.

> *Well, I'm disappointed. Who wouldn't be? With socks, a Sunday school shirt, some handkerchiefs, a hand-me-down sweater and a year's subscription to a religious magazine for children. The Little Shepherd. It makes me boil. It really does.*

How could we forgive ourselves for causing them so much heartbreak? Come off it! Just remember what they were like for the other 364 days of the year. It's therefore with some admiration that I quote this entry from the theatre critic James Agate's diary for 22 December 1939, where he refers to a refreshingly frank and honest letter sent to him from a friend in the country, who must surely be a distant cousin of mine.

> *There are six evacuated children in our house. My wife and I hate them so much that we have decided to **take away** something from them for Christmas!*

It's to that fighting spirit that I dedicate this book.

SCROOGE'S COUNTDOWN TO CHRISTMAS

Forward Planner

2 January
Freeze all leftover mince-pies, pudding and Christmas cake – though the cake will keep in the open air for at least eighty-three years without changing in either ~~taste~~ taste or appearance, which is why some small shopkeepers are still in business.

6 January
With Twelfth Night now past, you can safely pour any dregs from bottles of booze back into an all-purpose 'cocktail' bottle – usually this will originally have contained ginger wine or dark rum. Nothing yet discovered (with the possible exception of Chocolate Mint Liqueur) can ~~permanently~~ overpower the flavour of either of these beverages nor, for that matter, their ability to take the stains off pans.

7 January
* Collect and keep all Christmas cards – both leftovers and any 'spares'. Store these safely in carefully labelled boxes, along with any envelopes which could be re-used. Fold and conserve any wrapping paper, especially larger pieces which still have ribbon or rosettes attached to them.

8 January
Purchase as many presents as possible in the sales – handkerchiefs, gloves, scarves, boxes of stationery and any other universal item of rubbish. Also, Christmas cards will never be as cheap as they are now.

February
Start buying stocks of spirits and wines for Christmas drinking. Lock them away until the festive season.

Forward Planner

March

This is usually a cold, wintry month. Break off the padlock and start opening the booze you bought in February.

23 April

St George's Day and Shakespeare's birthday. Try to forget about Christmas, will you, for goodness' sake.

1 May

May Day, when maidens and young colts traditionally dance around the maypole. When this ridiculous spectacle is over, unwind the ribbons from the pole – these can be used later for decorations or wrapping special presents. Morris dancers tend to favour the ancient rite of 'go blotto' late in the day, so you may be able to persuade them to part with some bells or festoons, which will be perfect for Christmas.

June

Have your first Christmas panic attack now, but take heart because some coffin-dodging relatives are sure to ~~dearon~~ dearly depart' owing to the stress, and will thus leave you in peace over the festive season. Do, however, try to hide your glee at the funeral service.

❋ Watch Wimbledon to observe players' form, making stringent notes. In particular, look for those seeds who have gone to seed, then one week after finals day, nip down to your local sports shop and seek out their endorsed products. These are bound to be at half-price or less, and can make a suitable present for those with limited knowledge of tennis.

July

While you are on holiday, purchase a few local trinkets in the market in Cyprus or wherever you may be. These are utter crap and cost next to nothing, so make perfect presents for aunts and uncles. Particularly appreciated at Christmas-time are 'off-season' treats: summery items such as straw hats and little knick-knacks for the garden.

Forward Planner

August

A careful scrutiny of the top-ten US movies should enable you to pre-empt the tastes of youngsters this coming Christmas. In the past, hot telly- or film-related toys have included Star Wars figures, ET and Ninja Turtles. This trend-spotting should fill you with a lovely warm glow come December. Not because your own young relations are the only kids in their class with that year's top toy. They are not. You have made a fourfold profit by auctioning the desirable purchase to other desperate parents on Christmas Eve.

September

Buy books and CDs as presents. This will give you ample time to read the books and tape the CDs before you have to hand them over in December.

2 October

✱ Apply to have your credit card limits doubled and ✱ order two new chequebooks from your bank.

30 November

Traditionally 'stir-up Sunday' – while your neighbours are stirring their Christmas puddings ready for their traditional 'plum pudding coronary', you can stir up trouble by offering to take the children off their hands for the day, and explaining to the little treasures that there's no Santa Claus.

If you have unaccountably chosen to make some puddings this year, remember to add a generous handful of small coins – 5p is most suitable. This ensures that everyone gets a token of your goodwill, along with a chipped tooth.

Forward Planner

1 December
Buy Advent calendars. ~~open all~~ Open all the tiny windows, eat the chocolate figurines, then throw away.

9 December
Start stocking up on things that might come in handy over the holidays when unexpected presents are offered that might cause you to reciprocate: slippers, pipes, cherry brandy, dollies, chemistry sets, brooches, scent, Dairy Box, Cadbury's Milk Tray, etc.

15 December
Dig trenches, lay explosives and land-mines, erect a barbed-wire fence, purchase a supply of yacht sirens, maroons and flares ... in readiness for carol singers.

18 December
Set aside this day for baking. Uncle Ebenezer's crispy crunchy Mince-Pies are a speciality that I like to prepare for all my friends. The recipe — handed down lovingly from the original Uncle Scrooge — is similar to that for traditional mince-pies, but with the addition of 175 grams of coarse grit to the mincemeat mixture. This will be indistinguishable when thoroughly blended, but listen carefully when guests tuck in ... you're sure to hear those fillings going snap, crackle and pop!

24 December
Carefully label all presents received in the post. You can send them back next year with season's Greetings intact.

<u>25 December</u>
It's Christmas Day. If everything has gone according to plan, you should be left in perfect peace and total blissful isolation. Relish this brief, wonderful moment, as you will doubtless have few such joyful times throughout the coming year.

A CHRISTMAS CAROL

by Tom Lehrer

Christmas time is here, by golly
Disapproval would be folly
Deck the halls with hunks of holly
Fill the cup and don't say when.

Kill the turkeys, ducks and chickens
Mix the punch, drag out the Dickens
Even though the prospect sickens,
Brother, here we go again.

On Christmas day you can't get sore
Your fellow man you must adore
There's time to rob him all the more
The other three hundred and sixty four.

Relations sparing no expense'll
Send some useless old utensil
Or a matching pen and pencil,
'Just the thing I need, how nice.'

It doesn't matter how sincere it
Is, or how heart felt the spirit
Sentiment will not endear it,
What's important is the price.

Hark the herald Tribune sings
Advertising wondrous things

God rest ye merry merchants
May ye make the yuletide pay

Angels we have heard on high
Tell us to go out and buy

Let the raucous sleigh bells jingle
Hail our dear old friend Kris Kringle
Driving his reindeer across the sky
Don't stand underneath when they fly by.

PREPARATIONS

Before you start

Let me say right away that I'm absolutely at one with the late Duchess of Windsor when she said you can never have too many little black dresses. Not that I'm that way inclined, of course. I simply mean that, like Wallis, I too like to dispense valuable nuggets of advice that may help smooth some of the bumps and potholes along life's way. And let me begin right now by telling you that you can never start planning for Christmas too early. As a matter of fact, over the years, I have always tried to sneak a few quiet moments on Boxing Day when I can sit down with my wall chart and a brand-new diary for the coming year, to see exactly how best I can get myself ready for the rapidly approaching festive season. After all, with Sunday opening, there are going to be 363 shopping days that you'll need to avoid.

This level of forward planning may seem excessive when what you really want to be concentrating on are the summer holiday brochures that are plopping on to the doormat. But, seriously, you can't expect to ensure a miserable time all through next Christmas unless you have laid the ground very carefully in the fifty-one weeks leading up to it. Remember, if you put it off and put it off, then before you know it, St Andrew's Day will be just a blurry memory (well, it usually is for me, at any rate!) and you'll be opening the first of those envelopes with unfamiliar writing from an unrecognisable postmark, and from it you will take out a seasonal greeting signed by someone whose name you can't quite decipher, let alone remember. Whatever you do, don't panic.

Cards

It's the second week of August. There you sit with the patio doors flung back, a cup of tea the colour of liquorice in your hand because no one told you they'd put an empty milk carton back in the fridge, when, without a moment's bidding, you suddenly find yourself thinking the unthinkable.

What did you do with last year's Christmas card list?

And, you hear yourself saying, 'Why can't we be like Bill and Joan, and the minute we take the cards down, make a note of everybody who sent us one so that next year we don't waste time – or money – posting them to people like Phyllis in Carlisle, who we

met once on a Getting To Know You afternoon at that half-built hotel in Rhodes ... or was it Knossos?'

But why now? Why in the middle of a bloody heat wave? Why, when the reservoirs in Yorkshire might never for the next two centuries see their banks lapping with water? When even Sam's cactus collection looks as dry as Bernard Manning's cocktail cabinet on 1 January? Why do you know that you need to start preparing for Christmas this very day? Why? Because if you don't, you'll be sitting there on 19 December like last year, trapped between the last day for second-class postage and the last day for first-class, and having no choice but to put on the more expensive stamps, which costs you a good £6.36 over what it should have done if you'd got it together sooner. If only you'd had a list ...

Though where do you start with a Christmas card list? Whatever you do, do *not* try to send a card to everyone who sent you one last year ... the reason is simple. Most of them only sent you one because *you* sent *them* one, let's face it. So there's no way they're going to send you one this year, is there? The other perpetual truth about the Christmas card is that in even-numbered years – excluding leap years and those ending in 0 – you will finish up on 29 December with fifty-seven spare Christmas cards that you will have no use for. You will dutifully put them away with good intentions for using them up the following year. But by November will you be able to find them? No, because they will have gone where all single socks go, into that place of colossal darkness where Les Dennis is funny and tofu tastes nice. And in those years – odd numbers, excepting any prime numbers – you will have a postal delivery on 23 December which will include at least seven people you'd forgotten to send cards to. The local newsagent will have run out, the post office will have shut at lunch-time, and the garage will have nothing but cartoon cards featuring sex among reindeer, leaving you to explain over the next few weeks that (a) you'd been desperate to send them a card but had mislaid their address; (b) you know you sent the card over a week ago, and you are going to make a formal complaint to the shoddy outfit calling itself Royal Mail; (c) you put airmail stickers on some cards by mistake, so theirs is probably doing the rounds of a sorting office in Mauritius right now.

Here, then, are some golden rules: a Christmas Card list for people who don't care if they have no friends left by 29 December, and who would prefer to sever all relations with their family over the festive season.

1 Buy three different sizes of Tippex pen – you'll need the fine tip, especially if you want to make your signature fit over the squiggles on some of the cards you received last year. (Incidentally, whereas these pens offer none of the 'light-headedness' associated with the traditional little bottles of correction fluid, they do at least offer an outside chance of getting the white stuff where you want it.)

2 Having kept all the cards you received last year, you will have ample in both quantity and variety to re-use this year. Some points worth bearing in mind: try to find the sickliest 'baby Jesus' pictures to send to your atheist/Buddhist/Jewish friends; find anything featuring robins, snow or glitter to send to your most fashionable/trendy set. Next year, you can guarantee that these same middle-aged *Face* readers will send something similar, thinking, of course, that you were twelve months ahead of a major new trend.

3 There are two ways to recycle a card. The first way is quite simply to send the card exactly as you received it, merely adding below their signature 'and, of course, from John/Jenny' or whatever your name is. The recipient will think they've had double the value … *and* increased their friends twofold. Either that, or go the whole hog and cut the picture from the front of every card, and glue it to a fresh piece of blank white card. Frankly, though, I consider this far too much effort, and what's more it ends up looking as though you actually *bought* some new cards. Ridiculous waste of money!

4 A far more sensible approach is to create a new tradition. The Christmas card can become the Christmas postcard. Cutting off the front of those cards you received last year provides a newish unsoiled postcard ready for your greetings of the season. And if there are a few left over, simply take them on your summer holidays for use as a wacky 'Benidorm at Christmas' postcard!

5 If you really cannot face recycling last year's cards, you will need to enlist the help of your children (or someone else's children – these can be acquired relatively easily under cover of 'baby-sitting' or 'activity hour'). Each infant will have learned at school how to make a simple card, and once they have made one for each member of their own family, why not encourage them with a few Smarties to make up a dozen or so each for you. If this proves impossible, and you end up having to make them yourself, you should still *pretend* they were created by the young ones. What passes as endearing when produced by a six-year-old child seems plain amateurish and a little fey from a grown-up.

6 If you have neither the time nor the offspring for home-made cards, you must search out the smallest ones available. You may even use present-tags provided you can find an envelope to fit. However, this tactic has been known to backfire when the recipients think you've selected the cards because they were *cute* rather than because they were *cheap*.

7 Be wary of loading your cards with false promises. If you do not hope to see them in the New Year, then for goodness' sake don't write that you do. In fact, if there are certain individuals with whom you communicate exclusively by Christmas card, you should seriously consider striking them off your list, as you have obviously grown apart. Don't feel guilty; people change. Think of the savings to be made.

8 What's wrong with picking up a few 'boxed assortments' during the January sales? I tell you, I've been looking for a Biro refill (well, I refuse to buy a new one every time when the outer tube is perfectly sound apart from a few teeth-marks around one end) in W H Smith and seen a stampede of people buying up whatever's left. Do these sad specimens celebrate Christmas five days later than the rest of us? I've often asked myself. Or do they have a special place where they store stationery for eleven months, hoping the gum on the envelopes hasn't dried up, which will mean spending as much on Sellotape or glue as they previously saved on the cards! These people have no idea how to manage their hard-earned money. Either that, or they need to get out more!

9 When compiling your list, do not put your closest friends at the top – they'll never imagine they were deliberately left off, so any excuse for missing them out will be accepted. Tell them you've become absent-minded, and probably posted your cards in the paper recycling unit in the supermarket carpark instead of in the pillar box. (Men can blame this on nicotine patches – women can claim it's a side effect of HRT.) When it comes to family, despatch one card to a senior member of the household, and request that they send it on to all the other relations like a chain letter – if they want Christmas cards, let them pay the postage!!

10 Make sure business colleagues receive nothing but the bare minimum – a piece of folded memo paper with minimal greetings scrawled in spangly felt pen will do. Or a sheet of A4 from the recycling tray with 'Merry Christmas to All from Bill in Accounts' would be acceptable pinned to a strategic notice-board. Better still, why not take this opportunity to try out the office e-mail? You could 'post' a simple message right round the company without leaving your desk or dipping into your wallet. There's nothing worse than being thought generous or outgoing at this time of year … next thing, they'll be expecting you to buy drinks at the office party or

some such nonsense. If you are using the office franking-machine, stagger your despatch by sending only two or three a day, as this looks less suspicious than a huge pile of extra mail when your department usually sends out a couple of letters each week.

11 By now, you should have no more than a manageable dozen or so cards to send out. Which means you can easily avoid paying postage except where extreme distances are involved, or where you might not want them to see you pushing it through the letterbox in case they leap out and ask you in to share a schooner of Sanatogen. Don't hesitate to ask acquaintances or work colleagues to take a handful with them en route to and from home, rather like having your own private postal service. Where there seems no alternative to buying a stamp, do not be hasty! If it really does have to go by post, shove it discreetly in a postbox with absolutely no sign of a return address. Think of their excitement at the other end when the postman rings the bell early one morning, and the entire family rushes downstairs expecting a huge parcel … only to be charged excess postage for your recycled greeting. Superb!

12 These days there are free cards aplenty in cafés and reception areas of hotels and businesses – just stroll in and take a bundle. Never feel obliged to purchase anything. If these boobies are fool enough to give things away, then they must be expecting people to take them! Another good wheeze is to ring up some charities and suggest that you may be placing a large corporate order for five thousand cards, but you can't decide on the theme. Whoosh!! Next day your desk is covered in pristine samples, ready for you to inscribe. Of course, if you simply can't be bothered, tell everyone there was a wildcat strike at your local sorting office and the pillar boxes have been sealed up. This is extremely plausible these days.

Recently, I have noticed a trend creeping in from foreign parts, which I can heartily recommend. This involves sending out a very cheaply photocopied sheet of A4 paper with some scraps of information about your activities over the past year. One reason I endorse this American habit is that it is particularly vulgar, offensive and impersonal, and therefore is a refreshing antidote to the treacly sentiment that is usually allowed to pervade this ghastly season. Moreover, it resembles something like a school report or a medical record, and openly acknowledges the fact that you haven't been in touch since the previous December, and have absolutely no intention of changing this state of affairs until this time next year. For those of you unfamiliar with this 'newsletter' approach, allow me to point you in the right direction:

• Always begin the newsletter with details of your divorce, your children's accidents, your admissions to hospital for major surgery, family bereavements, etc.

• You may then light-heartedly move on to any pets that have met with unpleasant deaths or disasters.

• Try to include plenty of gossip … about your revolting neighbours, work colleagues who are having affairs, mutual friends who have recently been treated for a sexually transmitted disease, that kind of thing.

• Your friends will always enjoy reading about your new car, the swimming pool you're having installed, the jewellery you bought with the insurance money, a substantial inheritance, a small lottery win, etc. Nothing gives people more joy than sharing the joy of others.

• Try to avoid giving out your new address or telephone number as there is nothing worse than receiving unsolicited newsletters of this kind from distant acquaintances.

A final caution: there are still those who imagine that it saves time and money to take a small advertisement in the newspaper, announcing that this year you will not be sending cards, as you'll be making a charitable donation instead. Firstly, after paying the outrageous cost of this insertion, you will be reduced to begging for charity yourself. Secondly, you will spend twice as long as usual telephoning or sending notes to all your acquaintances to remind them to look in the newspaper for your advertisement. Utterly pointless.

DECORATIONS

The best advice for anyone forced to host the family Christmas is to hire a venue. In this way, you will avoid entirely any necessity to 'decorate' your home … which can often lead to redecoration after 6 January in my experience. A suitable site could be the village hall or the function room above a pub. Here there are often very pretty carpets of brown-and-orange swirls, in a sort of gravy-puddle-and-diced-carrot pattern – for rather obvious reasons. Better still, why not get hold of the keys to some vacant property on a light industrial estate? Just think: plenty of room for the kids to try out their bikes, rollerblades and skateboards, and at the end of the holiday season, the whole thing can be bagged up and hosed down (there are professional decontamination companies who are quite used to the kind of unpleasantness they are likely to encounter, so leave this sort of thing to them).

It's either that, or you condemn yourself to the expectation that you can somehow, in a matter of hours, transform your mid-terrace into something from Marks and Spencer's Christmas catalogue or a Winter Wonderland supplement in

Good Housekeeping – a happy home with a roaring log fire, a snoring golden retriever, ribbons and wreaths in perfect harmonies of green, red and gold, with presents round the base of a perfectly shaped tree that drips no needles, and brimming potpourris of dried oranges studded with cloves on every perfect side table. Don't kid yourself! Those images have as much to do with reality as the notion that Luciano Pavarotti is training for the pentathlon.

How I remember in my childhood years the supreme mystery of school Christmas decorations. For the last three weeks of term, classes seemed to consist of nothing more demanding than bringing in games or pets or licking the gummed ends of pre-cut strips of coloured paper, then carefully linking them with another piece, already glued, to make a multicoloured paper chain … which always had to be unpicked and started again when some halfwit like Jeffrey Sullivan put two pieces of the same colour next to each other. We kept ourselves amused for days, without ever thinking we were being ignored or exploited. Or there were the strange bags that arrived at the canteen late in the afternoon full of foil in peculiar forms which unravelled into great garlands of holes linked by regular silver shapes. It was only when one could eventually read the occasional remaining letters, 'ogenised pasteur' or 'eetings from your milkma', that we realised these were

simply the remnants from factories where they had pressed out the milk bottle tops. But how exotic such debris seemed. And not something your mother would ever find in Woolworths, however much you begged her to bring home something identical.

So, why not recapture childhood this year by using old magazines (I have always found the *Mail on Sunday* supplements perfect for this) or comics in a similar manner? Cut out regular pieces from each page, about six inches by two inches. Then use a *little* glue or Sellotape to bind the ends as you make a chain. Or thread a needle with some strongish cotton about ten feet in length. Along the length of the cotton, at regular intervals, place milk bottle tops by piercing them in the centre and threading them along. It's a good idea to wash them first, but do not throw the finished garland away after the season – keep it for use as a garden bird-scarer … then bring it in again in December, and so on ad infinitum. How your friends will applaud your ingenuity, and never stop remarking how much it reminds them of their childhood … yawn!

If, like me, you have a sweet tooth and a sour nature, there's a clever way of saving up for those extortionate dental charges that come round twice a year with the regularity of athlete's foot. Collect up sweetie wrappers instead of putting them in the bin, or hiding them under cushions! Fortunately, Cadbury's Roses and Quality Street are among the cheapest and brightest. You'll also need some foil containers from which you must wash any traces of the Chinese or Indian takeaways you have consumed throughout the year. Crinkle up the sweet wrappers in an artistic manner, and stick them to the cartons … or to anything you want … for a truly dazzling effect.

Or if it's silver tinselly stuff you're looking for, just go round the supermarkets well before Christmas. I guarantee you'll find special offers on aluminium roasting foil, something like 'three free metres with every roll'. Well, since it's obvious there's enough on every roll to insulate a loft without the 'three free metres', why not invest in one of these, then cut those three free metres off (off the top, silly, not the end) and shred them nicely in a mincer to create home-made angel-hair decorations. Couldn't be simpler.

Assuming you have access to a number of younger helpers, you might encourage them to start work on an advent crown – the kind that BBC's *Blue Peter* has been trying to get right since the days when Christopher Trace's pullover was the most racy thing on the small screen. Maybe, after all these years, it's time someone at home actually made one? So here goes, if my memory serves: the crown is essentially a 'mobile' consisting of a pair of wire coat hangers obtained free from the dry-cleaner's but beyond repair. In addition, you require a length of last year's tinsel and four candle stubs. It therefore brings together those not entirely symbiotic elements 'small children' and 'naked flames', and contravenes all natural laws of common sense, let alone the jurisdiction of the Health and Safety Executive. On balance, maybe you should just let them crack on with the paper-chain.

But, better than any of these, my all-time festive favourite is simply to collect together all the Christmas cards you have received, and to scatter them 'freestyle' face up on every visible horizontal surface throughout the house. You'll be amazed how far they go … there'll easily be enough even for teenagers' bedrooms where, as we know, uncluttered surfaces are especially hard to detect. Immediately, you will witness their instant decorative appeal, and marvel at these added benefits: no visitor in their right mind will try to lift a card (because you have carefully overlapped each one) to read who has sent it – something they invariably try to do when cards are 'roped' around mirrors or left standing on shelves and mantelpieces. And, in any case, they're only ever concerned about finding their *own* card, to make sure it's somewhere prominent and to remind themselves of their witty inscription. Far, far more rewarding, though, is going round the house on 6 January (although who's to stop you leaving them out until Easter? Eh!?) and carefully lifting them one by one so as not to disturb too much of the gathered dust, then congratulating yourself on having been able to keep the house clean without dusting any of your surfaces for weeks! What a sensational result, as my old friend David Coleperson (as we must learn to call him in these enlightened days) would say.

Of course, some die-hards may still insist on buying a tree. Why is this? Do these same boobies suddenly become all sparkly in the middle of May and say, 'Let's go

out and buy a Swiss cheese plant'? Have you ever heard any member of your family suggest it would be a thrill, for the month of August, to uproot a few rose bushes from the garden and stick them in a corner of the living room, where they will sit morosely obscuring the telly and desiccating next to the radiator? Reader, you have not. Remember that it was only thanks to that fool of a hen-pecked royal husband Prince Albert that this Scandinavian obsession invaded our hitherto sane island. Where are all the other Swedish habits we've adopted? Does anyone think it's pleasurable to spend a bank-holiday Monday queuing for the carpark at Ikea? How long can you stay in a sauna before it seems as though cardiac bypass surgery would be more fun? Do you know of anyone whose life has been improved by purchasing a pair of Sloggies? So, when it comes to allowing a six-foot spruce through the front door … think again. If you *must* erect a pole with lethal protrusions, make sure it contains nothing but man-made materials, extruded from petroleum by-products. Since Christmas is now almost totally artificial, why make an exception for the Christmas tree? Let's keep everything in glorious harmony, and allow nothing but plastic and nylon to decorate the house at this dismal time of year.

Or why not build your own? I guarantee that if you look in the kitchen cupboard or under the stairs, you'll find a worn-out Vileda floor mop, on which you were always intending to renew the sponge bit (why is it *never* the handle that goes?), which, when you go back to the shop where you bought it, turns out to be obsolete, necessitating purchase of a 'new, improved' model that does the same job at twice the price.

This will almost stand up of its own accord, assuming it has had around eight months to dry out and become as rigid as an ironing-board. At regular intervals down the pole, twist old wire coat hangers around the stem, and cover these in skeins of low-grade bobbly cotton wool, or – for added safety – some left-over wads of fireproof fibreglass loft insulation material. In the wrong light, some of your more senile house guests might mistake it for a display spinner of incontinence pads and panty-liners, but what do you care? The hoots of laughter there'll be when they try to insert an itch-inducing clump of rock wool in their rubber safety pants!

Whatever your choice of tree, you will be expected to 'dress' it, as though it were in need of some kind of modesty garment, indeed! If you're not sending out cards this year, then drape the ones you've collected up from last year all over the branches, with little gift tags from last year's presents hanging on the ends – you'll find most of the strings still attached to these, saving lots of effort and cash. More elaborate tree decoration is both time-consuming and utterly pointless. Consider the following alternative: on Christmas Eve (no sooner, for this is a somewhat unsightly stratagem) you should gather up a bundle of broken baubles and offcuts of tinsel and so on that you were thinking of throwing out. Then, standing a minimum of four feet from your target, hurl the whole lot towards the tree. However this lands, however much sticks, just leave it all as it is. The next day, when the family arrives, you will have prepared an exceptionally plausible tale about how the vile cat from three doors down raced through your hall twenty minutes ago when you had the front door open and flung itself up to the top of the tree, as cats are wont to do (though not even Desmond Morris quite understands why). With a tear in your eye, you will proceed to explain how – after all the hard work you had put in, not going to bed until 3 a.m. – you haven't been able to face the refurbishment. I can assure you, you will barely manage to finish the sentence before the whole congregation have thrown off their cardies and got down to work on a full-scale repair and a new arrangement (which will scarcely improve on yours).

Then, there's the question of Christmas tree lights. Reader, every January when you take these down from the tree and put them away in a cardboard box, they are working perfectly. Eleven months later, when you take them out of the box and plug them in, they do not work. When you go round to the electrical shop, they tell you these are obsolete, but that they have in stock the most fantastic twinkling, winking lights that are computer-controlled and respond to the human voice, the climate and the days of the week. Enough! Do not purchase any more tree lights. There is a solution in sight. Somewhere in view of your garden, there is probably a tower block whose unfortunate residents have neither a garden nor even a window box. Think of the joy you will bring them by having a beautifully lit outdoor tree flashing away in your garden. All they have to do, you inform them generously, is club together to buy the lights and pay for the electricity, then you will be extremely benevolent and allow them to watch the lights from their windows, while enjoying the full benefit yourself from much closer quarters. At the end of the season, offer to store the lights for them. By next year, they'll have moved on or forgotten, leaving you with a fine set of outdoor lanterns.

On the inside, some households do seem unable to outgrow the habit of decking the halls with boughs of holly, which I have always found a most inhospitable house guest, forever inflicting nasty scratches on you as you wander past at night on your way to the fridge or the downstairs loo. What's more, when it occurs naturally in the garden, dripping with delicious (and slightly toxic!) red berries, it is often jealously guarded by mean homeowners, and can be very painful to pick from your neighbour's tree, necessitating the berry-hunter leaving home armed with secateurs, gardening gloves, and strong plastic bags. Ivy is far simpler, should you really desire a natural-looking shred of greenery indoors, and is far easier to steal from gardens, graveyards, etc. Some varieties do produce a nasty rash when in contact with human skin. Ensure this is the kind you obtain, especially if you intend to use it as a table decoration or as a garnish on the turkey.

For those who feel no table is decorated until it is festooned with crackers, here are my tips. Assuming that you have an average family (does anybody?), then you'll probably use at least twenty-four toilet rolls in the course of the year. The inner cardboard roll will serve as the 'log' part of your crackers. Add to these about a dozen kitchen roll inners, which will be used for the 'superior' crackers. (Although these contain exactly the same rubbish as the smaller crackers, some ignorant guests will be fooled into thinking they've gone one better than the person sitting next to them. This is rather pathetic, but then that's human nature for you.) Into these you can stuff whatever you wish, though I recommend a hat made from folded pages of the *TV Times*, which are more colourful than standard newspapers, added to which this is one magazine you will have no desire to keep back copies of lying around the house. As a gift, I find that books of matches taken from restaurants can add quite a 'bang' to proceedings, but for the more nervous, perhaps a live mouse or a couple of sleepy wasps, which will be extremely energetic once the cracker is pulled and they see the light of day. Each cracker will also need a joke, so here are my favourites:

What has four legs and flies?
When it is stuck up!

What's green and goes hith?
Shylock Holmes.

How do you hire a car?
Dung.

Why did the chicken cross the road?
Because it would quack up.

How do you join the Army?
Because it brakes (breaks).

And so on. In fact, I'm tittering a bit myself just imagining the total lack of mirth around the table. Next, you need to wrap the filled cracker tube with some coloured paper – toilet paper is quite acceptable. Twist the ends, and that's it. Your guests will utter shrieks of delight when they find there's no bang and no silly 'brainteaser' puzzle to annoy them all through Christmas. These will be the smoothest crackers they have ever pulled!

To add some final touches, let me suggest a couple of easy ways to create that indoor 'winter landscape' look. Firstly, there is a method guaranteed to infuriate the ladies of the house (who tend, in my experience, to do most of the vacuuming!), but which will delight the little ones. All it requires is for someone 'accidentally on purpose' to let off the fire extinguisher – though it's not much use

if it's the water variety! – and
hey presto, an instant snowfall of
a couple of inches. However, if
later in the day there is a nasty
accident with those chestnuts
roasting on an open fire, then the
last laugh could be on you. A more
safety-conscious method is the
cunning plan of stealing Uncle
Toby's bottle of Head & Shoulders.
This should result in a snowfall
to rival a ski resort all through
the holidays.

And don't forget to bring joy
into the lives of your neighbours
and all those who pass your
door at this special time of year.
It is very easy to hang a wreath
from a doorknocker or a nail,
and there is no difficulty in
finding very pretty red-and-
green wreaths left over from
Remembrance Day. These
should be removed from
cenotaphs and memorials as soon
as possible after 11 November to
avoid them spoiling in the rain. If
you prefer something more floral, a
visit to the churchyard or local
crematorium should provide what
you are looking for.

An Atrocious Institution

by George Bernard Shaw

Like all intelligent people, I greatly dislike Christmas. It revolts me to see a whole nation refrain from music for weeks together in order that every man may rifle his neighbour's pockets under cover of a ghastly pretence of festivity. It is really an atrocious institution, this Christmas. We must be gluttonous

because it is Christmas. We must be drunken because it is Christmas. We must be insincerely generous; we must buy things that nobody wants, and give them to people we don't like; we must go to absurd entertainments that make even our little children satirical; we must writhe under venal officiousness from legions of freebooters, all because it is Christmas – that is, because the mass of the population, including the all-powerful middle-class tradesman, depends on a week of licence and brigandage, waste and intemperance, to clear off its outstanding liabilities at the end of the year. As for me, I shall fly from it all tomorrow or next day to some remote spot miles from a shop, where nothing worse can befall me than a serenade from a few peasants, or some equally harmless survival of medieval mummery, shyly proffered, not advertised, moderate in its expectations, and soon over. In town there is, for the moment, nothing for me or any honest man to do.

PRESENTS

Nothing can be more important at this time of year than choosing the correct gift for those you hate to love. You have but a single chance to get it wrong on this one day of the year, so woe betide any of you who make the appalling mistake of actually *buying* something the recipient likes … or worse, something they might *want*. There are countless ways to avoid this, and I have time to offer you only a few scraps of advice handed down from Glaswegian great-grandfathers to great-grandsons, or gleaned over the years spent in the more poorly paid reaches of the acting profession.

Firstly, do not prevaricate. You may as well start deciding on your gift purchases as early as possible … say around the second week of January when things have calmed down, and the sales are in full swing. A study of our Christmas shopping habits was recently published by a psychologist, showing that people who leave their shopping to the last moment come out worst. Not only is their taste in presents likely to be worse, but they are accused of being depressed and neurotic, lacking self-confidence and suffering from high social anxiety. Late shoppers also become criminally cunning in their employment of excuses, often lying when they say they are far too busy at work or there's too much to do at home. Apparently, this is just a feeble attempt to confound accusations that they are disorganised or incompetent. This is definitely the book for them!

There is, is there not, a law of diminishing returns when it comes to Christmas presents? Allow me, if you will, to take you back a mere four years, through which to examine the curious ritual performed between a mature male (myself) and his equally mature sibling rival (my sister). Let us call it the 'gifting rite'. In 1994, I offer my sister a £135 headscarf from Hermès, perhaps in the vain hope that it will make her look a little more like Princess Margaret and a little less like Hilda Ogden. My sister retaliates with a book of recipes by Keith Floyd. (I, who have yet to have a plug fitted to the microwave, should be given a cookery book … I ask you!) By 1995, I am giving my sister a pair of tickets to *Miss Saigon*, while she provides me with a pair of socks. One year on, and my sister is the recipient of a bottle of Dior's Poison (ha ha) purchased duty-free in Los Angeles. In return, I am given a photograph of her new grandchild. This year, I shall offer my sister a copy of my book – unsigned, need I add. I expect to settle down on Christmas morning to unwrap a jar of her least-successful damson jam, still not set four months on. Next year, when she asks whether we should continue to exchange presents at Christmas, I shall have no hesitation in replying: 'Why not! I always exchange yours.'

And this is how the whole sham will eventually wither, until Christmas is no more celebrated than Whitsun or the Assumption. Where Easter is already little more than a chocolate egg and a few bunnies, 25 December will be a day when we prise open a few selection boxes, and wonder what to do until the day after Boxing Day. The birth of a former guru called Jesus will become little more than a hazy memory of green Brut bottles and wallets just too small to take twenty-pound notes, stuffed with cardboard credit cards that fooled nobody.

Then, there's the other route, which is to phone up everybody you know and ask them outright what they want. This is sure to provoke great embarrassment, and the hasty condemnation of the whole hateful commercial business at this time of year. This lets you off the hook at once, since you can say that you feel exactly the same way, and you were so relieved that you both saw eye to eye on something at last. But do not be fooled if a group of friends all loudly agree that they will spend no more than five pounds on each other this year. When this happened to me, I was astonished when one party in the group became extremely irritable with his beloved. He, you see, had opened a medium-sized parcel on Christmas morning, exquisitely wrapped, containing nothing more than a photograph frame, with a black-and-white portrait of his sweetheart. His heart sank. 'But, when we agreed five pounds, I didn't mean *you*,' he squealed, looking on as she unwrapped gift after expensive gift!

Unfortunately, if you are catering for little ones, the problem is far greater. For anyone unfamiliar with the modern child, permit me to offer a simple pointer. Forget the idea of a Christmas stocking. This was suppressed at least ten years ago when pillowcases became the common currency on the average bedstead. Today, even double duvet covers are not unheard of where very greedy children – or very stupid parents – live! The argument being that, if Father Christmas *is* going to deliver that computer you promised them, how the hell is he going to squeeze it into a stocking?! Also, you can disabuse yourself of the fanciful notion that any child will squeal with delight, as we once gratefully did, at the sight on Christmas morning of an orange and a bag of nuts. Nowadays, a mountain bike is the starting point for negotiation, and many children are so inundated with gifts that they are still opening parcels from dawn till dusk well into the New Year.

The
ANTI-SANTA CAMPAIGN

HELP US FIND A WAY TO GUARANTEE SANTA NEVER DARKENS *YOUR* CHIMNEY AGAIN

New members must carry out at least four of the following ten acts to stamp out unwanted Santas to qualify:

- Leave him a salad with low-calorie yoghurt dressing, suggesting that if he partakes of any more mince-pies and sherry, he'll never get into that silly red twinset this time next year.

- Casually leave open a copy of a veterinary dictionary at the page for 'Reindeer: Cases of BSE'.

- Have the chimney cleaned, then rediscover the joys of a real coal fire.

- Steal the sleigh and dump the burned-out shell on a nearby industrial estate. You can blame joyriders.

- Start up a petition against low-flying reindeer.

- Install a simple gin trap in the hearth — the inhumane version that routinely provokes moral outcry will serve you best for this purpose.

- Insulate the chimney with a protective coating of tar and feathers.

- Buy a Rottweiler, and leave a 10 x 8 colour photograph of Santa near its food bowl.

- Move into a block of flats.

- Leave corn plasters or verruca patches in the stockings.

APPLICATION FORM

- -

YES! I WOULD LIKE TO JOIN **The ANTI-SANTA CAMPAIGN.**

NAME: . . . .

ADDRESS: . . . .

. . . .

. . . .

AGE: (MUST BE OVER 8) . . . .

SEND TO PO BOX 25, 12 REINDEER WAY, STAGSHIRE, UK

JOIN TODAY

For my part, when it comes to buying gewgaws for children, I have always found the ideal present is the most mouthwatering: a large cardboard box, beautifully wrapped, containing a second box, even more brightly wrapped and decorated, within which is another box, and so on, until at least six boxes are tightly packed inside each other. There's no need to put anything in the smallest box, as over the years I've noticed that children just like pulling parcels to pieces. They won't even notice by the time they've reached the last container. Or give them my classic children's present of all time: batteries, toys not included. Well, it saves all that tearful charging round twenty-four-hour garages hoping they've got the type you need to make your new 'Wetty Betty' do her wee-wee. And anyway, it's so easy to get these things utterly wrong. I mean, is it Powder Strangers this year, or is it My Little Peony?

If you are a grandparent, or have grown a little out of touch through premature senility, there are some basic facts that you need to grasp about young people and presents. Firstly, you must understand that each year will have its 'big toy'. In recent years, for instance, we have had Tracy Island, which sounds like a weather girl, but is in fact a kind of housing association for toy soldiers.

Anyhow, the provision of this principal item is the responsibility of the parent or guardian, while other family members, right the way down to the remotest 'uncle' or 'aunt' totally unconnected by any trace of DNA, are encouraged to buy the accessories. For example, if this year's hot toy is a Baywatch Babe (now, why would I dream up such a thing?), then the parents would buy the Pamela Anderson doll itself … rather top-heavy, one imagines. A caring grandpa might like to purchase her a new bikini set, and offer to spend the afternoon making sure it fits. And me? Well, I would provide a stretch of Californian beach – i.e. a bucket of sand. It scarcely matters anyway because you can be sure that by Christmas lunchtime Baywatch Babe will have gone missing, last seen swimming in the murky blue waters down by the U-bend.

What's even worse than getting kiddies the 'wrong' toy is not realising how old your children or grandchildren are. Wasn't it John Betjeman who was given a terrible ticking off by a friend of his for missing his god-daughter's birthday?

Without a moment's hesitation, he went out and bought her a huge doll. A few days later, he rang to ask if all was well, and whether the present was just what she wanted. 'Not exactly,' complained the mother. 'Your god-daughter is a headmistress now.'

Of course, there is no universally agreed, elegant method of accepting a gift that you have unwrapped in horror, knowing that it's the last thing you'd ever have bought yourself, even if it was one of only two things left in Harrods and the other was a Ronco Buttoneer. To some extent, this is a throwback to that first-ever Christmas back in Bethlehem. Think about it a moment. How would you react if some distant relatives you hadn't set eyes on in *years* bought you and your little tot a herd of livestock? Needless to say, your first thought would be that they were after something in return, after which you'd force one of those polite 'you shouldn't have' smiles, and attempt to push the assorted health risks into a quiet corner of the house where they would be gradually forgotten about by the time those very first Christmas cards were taken down. Mind you, it works both ways. You could hardly picture yourself turning up at the stable with gold, frankincense and a three-pack of white tube sox, now could you?

If in doubt, particularly where people like brothers-in-law and nephews are concerned, have no inhibitions about proffering a beautiful leather-look diary with gold metallic corners, gilded page edges and an elegant braided bookmark ... and the name of your petrol station embossed on the front. Or how about a calendar for the current year? These are available at absolutely knock-down prices, since there are only four weeks to run (though some do provide the month of January for the following year at no extra charge). Ditto with diaries – which can, of course, be used, with a little adjustment, throughout the coming twelvemonth. Such a slip in offering somebody the outgoing year, if noticed by the recipient, can be laughed off, without a trace of embarrassment, as an endearing oversight, or an eccentricity, or – if you are a proficient liar – with considerable anger, and threats to go back to the shop the very next day and have the young single mother who served you sacked on the spot. This should be enough to have any weak-willed person's heartstrings playing 'Climb Ev'ry Mountain', and pleading with you not to do anything so inconceivably cruel, and what does it matter anyway, a diary's a diary, no matter what year is stamped on the outside.

In fact, it's worth me pointing out to you that unused diaries actually acquire vintage status, and are still immensely useful. They should never be thrown away, since, owing to the cyclical nature of the Gregorian calendar, the diary is identical every few years or so. For example, the calendar for 1998 is the same as that for 1987 and for 1981. So now you could find a very handy use for the 1981 diary …

What I call 'real' books are probably a bit of a mistake ... except, of course, if you are thinking of giving this one!! I do tend to find that people often give each other the same book, since there are always a few bestsellers that are piled high in very attractive positions at the front of bookshops. This is so that you can lazily cross a dozen names off your list simply by taking a handful of them over to the very handily nearby cash desk. It's only when you get home that you realise you've bought everyone a copy of *Theatrical Anecdotes that Could Easily Have Happened at Christmas* by Ned Sherrin ... which seems very similar to something you gave them all last year ...

Stocking-fillers are never a problem in my house. What could be simpler than to fill a stocking with all those free shampoos and soaps you've collected over the years from hotels and aeroplanes? And for special people, throw in one or two of the miniature bottles of wine or spirits they give you during the flight – because these are made of plastic, there's no chance of a nasty accident down in the toe! I also make a point, during the course of the year, of buying anything that is offered as 'three for the price of two'. This means that, if you give away the third item each time, you'll have been able to offer Christmas presents to all and sundry without it costing you a penny! Not even a Tory MP could have dreamed up such creative accounting, I'm sure, and it's something of which I'm extremely proud.

Another nice gesture is to redirect any subscriptions to unwanted publications you may have, for there are many deserving acquaintances who don't yet know the pleasure of receiving six copies of every Innovations catalogue, or the chance to enjoy the lovely gifts available from Past Times or from Valentines' Adult Toys Emporium. This would bring both colour and joy to their humdrum lives, and will be a gift they can be reminded of throughout the year when, every third week, a new set of fabulous brochures cascades on to the doormat.

A number of other cunning techniques can be employed to ensure that as little as possible is paid for gifts ... or preferably nothing at all. The key to success is also to make sure that the basic scam lies undetected for as long as possible. For instance, why not give every member of your family, and possibly even some of your closest friends, three CDs each? This may, at first sight, appear ludicrously extravagant, or even mad, but you will have obtained the discs by signing up each person for the introductory offer of a music 'club', as seen advertised on every piece of paper that ever falls out of the *Radio Times*. The first three records or cassettes are always free, and by the time the full price has to be paid, then the obligation to continue membership will rest with the lucky recipient. In many ways, you could be seen to have done them a great service by opening their minds to a selection of Vera Lynn classics or Sounds of the Seventies which might otherwise have passed them by.

Another rather nice, personalised item can be created with little more than careful forward planning and a blank video cassette. All you need to do is record the end-of-year *Newsnight* review, though there are many other variants to choose from. Store these tapes for a number of years, and then pass them off as a special anniversary video of that year … which ought to coincide with something anniversary-ish in that person's life, such as the year they had their verruca removed, or the year they were mugged while on holiday in Florida. Along similar lines, it can be very prudent to buy a newspaper on the day of birth whenever there's a happy addition to your extended family. Carefully file the newspaper in a safe place for around twenty years, then give it as a lavish present, fooling the recipient into thinking you have purchased a very expensive, specially 'yellowed' facsimile.

Dangerous dolls take flight

By Nigel Bunyan

PARENTS were warned yesterday about a Flying Angel Christmas toy that can cause serious injury when it breaks up in flight.

The doll which is supposed to fly like a helicopter after being activated by a drawstring, has been shown to hurl fragments around a room at up to 90mph.

Daily Telegraph 29/11/96

Two suggestions for that very difficult age group – adolescent boys – which are bound to go down well are these. First, take a little poke around your attic, where I'm sure you'll find some odd carpet offcuts or, if you're very lucky, some complete squares or carpet tiles. These can simply be offered to the lad with the explanation that you've heard they're the very latest, exotic Subbuteo soccer pitch. Well, you've seen the patterns they cut in the grass these days, haven't you? The same boys always seem to like to have the most up-to-date national team soccer strip. Now this can be difficult, since in order to be really 'with it', you'll need to visit your kit supplier every two hours which is the maximum interval allowed before they redesign it in completely different colours. Instead of this wasted effort, visit some charity clothing shops, where you'll discover an abundance of recent strips, hardly worn but discarded by fashion-crazy youth. Keep these for around ten to fifteen years, then offer them as 'vintage' soccer shirts. You'll be adored.

These days I tend occasionally to eat in restaurants where, like me, you may have noticed that near the cash desk, they often place a bowl of free mints or some other kind of sweeties. During the course of the year, take a handful with you each time you leave an establishment, and you'll be *astonished* how many gifts these can be turned into. Just ignore the statistics about each mint being coated in an average of seven different strains of urine. After all, *you're* not going to be eating them, are you?

In this era of conservation and ecology, there should be less shame attached to the notion of recycling the odd unwanted gift or ten. For instance, try putting in a row, on Boxing Day, all the assorted bath oils, soaps and cheap scents you've been given. Your house will look like a branch of Timothy White's, I guarantee. Now, try to work out which of those gaily coloured bottles has been recycled. Not the glass, you twit! I mean, which of the donors has passed on an unwanted flacon of *Fragrance de Chat Tom* or a demister full of *FU2*? Or that plastic bottle of Body Shop 'Broccoli and Horseradish Foot Smear' which is still in its original raffia presentation nest, hand-made by unexploited Amazonian tribal virgins? You can't tell, can you? Point taken? Some items are just *made* for passing on – and it doesn't have to be done the next day. Here is my list of non-perishable goods that can be redistributed, without worrying about whether the size is right, because the price certainly is!

• Perfume
• Soap
• Books
• Magazine subscriptions (just send them a change-of-address card)
• Gift vouchers
• Bottles of booze (though you'd be a fool to do it)
• Money (ditto, very much so)
• Anything electrical (other than *very* personal items where size matters)
• Anything practical (knives, cans of motor oil, etc.)
• Boxer shorts and socks (unworn if possible)

And here's a list of items that can also be shuffled around from Edna to Edward, with the proviso that you make a note of the sell-by date on the *outside* of the parcel, in case you don't actually need to hand on all the dozens of presents you'll be given this year:

• Boxes of chocolates
• Sides of smoked salmon
• Tins of caviar (how could you think of letting this one out of your sight?)
• Pets (worth remembering that a rabbit over a year old won't have much life in it, whereas a puppy can easily reach its third birthday before anyone will think it's an old mutt, assuming of course that you make sure it still isn't house-trained). And don't forget, pets are not just for Christmas, they can be given at Easter or Whitsun or for christenings, etc., etc.
• Meat products (best to destroy these immediately in any case; no one wants to be accused of wilful manslaughter)
• Fruit & veg (people give you *these* for Christmas?)

Arguably my finest hour, when it comes to saving money on presents, was the year when I purchased for every one of my friends and family a bottle of Corton-Charlemagne 1986, which was on special offer at fifteen bottles for the price of twelve. Each bottle was carefully wrapped and labelled, and awaited the recipients underneath the boughs of the Christmas tree. After lunch, everyone took their parcel with unbounded anticipation, ready to rip open the wrapping paper. At this point, I rushed into the room, announcing that I had just heard the news on the radio and there was an urgent product recall on certain bottles of wine. I offered to check one of the batch codes on a sample bottle, and … sure enough, it was tragically one of the contaminated shipment. Each bottle would have to be carefully wrapped in a cloth and placed in a cool place as soon as possible to avoid danger. What could I do, but protect my guests from exploding glass, and return the bottles after Christmas on their behalf? They were greatly relieved, and my cellar was well stocked through until May! Another way of achieving the same effect is by carefully preparing a sinister-looking product recall announcement on your word-processor, then pretending you have cut it out of yesterday's newspaper (do not make the mistake of saying 'today's' newspaper, as these are not published on Christmas Day). To ensure success, remember to give everyone the same present! Or at least the same shape when wrapped – for instance, CDs or books. And do please make sure that you want to keep the CDs or books for yourself, otherwise the point of the exercise is somewhat wasted.

Finally, you could always give money. I've no doubt it'll be the cheapest thing you can find at this time of year.

> ## TITANIC TOME
> AN early prize for tastelessness in Christmas books goes to Last Dinner on the Titanic. With recipes and menus from the ship's five-star restaurant, "this lavishly illustrated gift book includes suggestions for music, serving and decorations". Let's hope it sinks without a trace.
>
> **Times 13/11/96**

Christmas boxes

One sure way to spread happiness among the lower orders throughout the month of December is by handing out Christmas boxes to your domestic staff, such as the gardener, the cleaning lady, nanny and cook. And don't forget working people like the postman, the dustman, the newsagent, the paper-boy, the florist, the chemist, the grocer and the men who dig up the road outside the house at 8 a.m. on Sunday mornings. To all these lovely folk, I like to give an envelope, and watch their eyes light up with pleasure as they imagine the twenty-pound note I have secreted inside. Really, you know, money is too crass an offering at this time of year, when what you are looking for is something to show quite how much you care. Naturally, they are all far too polite to open their gift in front of me, so it's only when they arrive home that they discover my personal Christmas bonus consists of a lovely illustrated card featuring a lily of the valley with a prayer printed over it, usually with a moral about the need to avoid greed, jealousy and covetousness, and to be generous to those in need. These make excellent bookmarks, and are available free on the tables at the back of Catholic churches throughout the country. A present with real usefulness, I'm sure you'll agree.

It is a dangerous oversight forget to offer these small ezzies, which can mean a eat deal to the lower rders. One disastrous year omitted to give the annual reat to the paper-boy, who etaliated most unpleasantly by reneging on our confidential little delivery arrangements. You can imagine my horror when, in the third week of January, he casually posted my monthly copy of *Big Bouncy Blondes on Beaches* straight through the family letterbox, having deliberately removed it from its protective brown-paper wrapper. This is the kind of thing one wishes to avoid, and indeed *can* avoid, by careful use of a little goodwill.

Gifts for pets

Those of us who love our little furry pussies or our gerbils might also want to offer them a little something at this time of year. This is perfectly understandable, and nothing to be ashamed of. But you must not weaken. What is the point in buying a stocking for your dog, when all it contains is a few biscuits and a squeaky plastic pudding? He will not be impressed, believe me. What the dog wants is one of those things he's seen on the telly when he's been watching his canine chum from *Neighbours* – something that he believes all the other dogs on his patch will be getting. Those dogs are the pampered result of pathetic owners, and will see through any elaborate attempt to buy their affections. Owners such as these deserve to be given a copy of an invaluable guide I found on my travels, entitled *Puppy Care for Beginners* by the Hong Kong Restaurateurs' Association. My recommendation for a pet present is foolproof, as no dog or cat has ever, to my knowledge, complained. All you need do is save up the leftover mince-pies, sprouts, bits of pudding and so on. Wrap these in old newspaper – or, if you must, gift wrap that is beyond re-use – and present them to the pet on 27 December. Pets do not keep diaries, so will not be aware that they are two days behind everyone else. However, for peace of mind, it might be worth putting any calendars well out of reach of the dog basket for a while.

FATHER AND SON

by Edmund Gosse

On Christmas Day of this year
1857 our villa saw a very unusual sight. My
father had given strictest charge that no difference
whatever was to be made in our meals on that day; the
dinner was to be neither more copious than usual nor less so. He
was obeyed, but the servants, secretly rebellious, made a small plum-
pudding for themselves. (I discovered afterwards, with pain, that Miss
Marks received a slice of it in her boudoir.) Early in the afternoon, the maids
– of whom we were now advanced to keeping two – kindly remarked that 'the
poor dear child ought to have a bit, anyhow,' and wheedled me into the kitchen,
where I ate a slice of plum-pudding. Shortly I began to feel that pain inside which
in my frail state was inevitable, and my conscience smote me violently. At length I
could bear my spiritual anguish no longer, and bursting into the study I called out:
'Oh! Papa, Papa, I have eaten of flesh offered to idols!' It took some time, between
my sobs, to explain what had happened. Then my father sternly said: 'Where is
the accursed thing?' I explained that as much as was left of it was still on the
kitchen table. He took me by the hand, and ran with me into the midst of the
startled servants, seized what remained of the pudding, and with the
plate in one hand and me still tight in the other, ran till we reached
the dust-heap, when he flung the idolatrous confectionery on to
the middle of the ashes, and then raked it deep down into the
mass. The suddenness, the violence, the velocity of
this extraordinary act made an impression on my
memory which nothing will ever efface.

ENTERTAINING

FOOD

Unless you are in a position to have Christmas delivered in a sealed basket from Harrods (once the exclusive privilege of a few Tory MPs with a passion for asking questions), then your preparations will inevitably include a trip to the supermarket. This requires much careful forethought, for if Sunday mornings encourage inexperienced drivers on to the road as sun encourages flowers to bloom, then a superstore in pre-Christmas week is enough to bring out every D-registered Ford Fiesta and Honda Civic within a fifty-mile radius.

If you happen to be an inexperienced supermarket shopper who hasn't seen all that Dale Winton has to offer, the first thing that will strike you is the sheer size of these things (no, not Dale Winton's). As you stand at the automated entrance, you are unlikely to be able to see to the other end of the shop ... or even to the sides. This is quite normal, and has to do with the curvature of the Earth. Then, as you enter the store, swept along on a wave of wheeled trolleys, you will encounter an array of chill cabinets. Beware, for these are layered as a trap for the inexperienced purchaser. Many, if not all, items will be marked with a gaudy sticker in letters big enough for the hard-of-seeing 'Christmas Special', and might include canapés, crudités, dips and hors d'oeuvres – all daintily wrapped, all frighteningly expensive and all completely unnecessary. You will observe countless shoppers (many holding responsible management positions in real life) standing transfixed by the variety, and finding themselves quite unable to choose. These men – for they *will* be men – may have entered the store as much as two hours ago, and yet they have progressed no more than fifteen feet. To avoid becoming part of this undisciplined throng, you must avert your eyes, and plough on towards the sparsely populated aisle of toiletries and household goods at the workaday end of the store.

Once you have secured your handful of essentials, you are free to roam. Here, it is vital to remember that all these shoppers are on the same mission impossible. Assuming you are not in the most 'downmarket' of local establishments, each – like you – will have prepared their list from *Delia Smith's Winter Collection*, and therefore each will be sourcing exactly the same ingredients. So why spend hours searching for the fresh cranberries or the corn-fed chicken when you have just seen a perfectly adequate supply wheeled right past your nose? After all, until these goods are swiped at the checkout, they're free to be swiped by you!

Whatever you choose for your main meal, it's worth stocking up for those unexpected arrivals who ring the bell unannounced at 5 p.m. on Boxing Day. To make sure they don't outstay their welcome, you could purchase a selection of hardy stand-bys, as shown on this list.

The minute your booty is secured, lose no time in heading directly for the checkout. Now, a gentle word of warning. It really is unlikely that you will get away with the 'ten items or fewer' line on a day like this, but it is always worth a go if you have anything less than, let's say, twenty-five, and put on a downcast and dejected air that suggests you might

```
 2   Tinned pears and apricots

 1   Evaporated milk

 1   Pilchards

 1   Ginger nuts

 1   Anchovies

 1   Icing sugar

 1   Skimmed milk powder

 1   Meringue cases

 1   Brazil nuts

 1   Polony

 1   Jar of instant lemon tea

24   Peach toilet roll
     (also for use as napkins)


    ******************
    Supermarket Co. Ltd.
    VAT 123 4567 89123
    ******************
```

suffer a mild stroke if you don't reach the
exit before much longer. If
unsuccessful, you must press on,
but don't just look at the
length of the queues, study
the personnel! You are
looking for an ambitious,
acned youth, keen to
'maximise throughput'.
This boy is determined to
be a manager before he is
twenty-five. Be aware of
the telltale signs: the beads
of sweat or a low-level hum
which will reach you without
the aid of hearing.

When you have chosen the correct
queue, you need to approach each of the
customers ahead of you, and suggest that they might let you go in front of them
because you 'haven't got much'. At the same moment, you should barge your way
past and turn your back firmly on the person immediately behind. This being a
British supermarket, it is highly unlikely that you'll detect even a murmur of
protest. Though do be careful, as the time of year can do funny things to middle-
aged ladies' temperaments (I think it's something in their replacement
hormones), and as a further caution, beware tattoos: they are not a welcoming
sign, on men or women!

Having put this ordeal firmly behind you, knowing that you will not need to
repeat it for at least fifty-one weeks, you will arrive home with around thirty-eight
carrier bags – some heaving, some almost empty. In effect, it is at this point that
you will discover whether you have bought enough food to see a family of eight
through until the summer solstice, or whether you have come back with only half

the things you required, and now have to work out how to divide fifteen sprouts between seventeen guests. But have no fear. Firstly, there is obviously not enough room in your kitchen to store everything in those carrier bags. Anything temperature-sensitive can be put into the refrigerator. Anything with a looming sell-by date should be eaten before anybody turns up to spoil your fun. Anything remaining must be hidden temporarily under the bed, but well out of reach of any pets.

Now, collect together all the empty carrier bags, and proceed to tear large holes in the bottom of them. Next, place these in the back garden – some hanging from the fence, others on the ground. A few stray bits of food wrapping, or the odd empty cream carton, will help in your endeavour. The result should look fairly trashy, as though a fox has been in your garden and devoured everything you left out there ... and thus, when your guests arrive on Christmas Day to find you in tears, you point to the devastation beyond the back-door, and sob, 'Foxes ... everything .... gone ... what to do?' Their pity will be so overwhelming that they will comfort you, and suggest that you all repair to the nearest large luxury hotel, where they will pay for everything. It will be the best meal you ever had.

If, on the other hand, you have doubts about their generosity stretching to this, then remember that you will have to start kitchen preparations about six days before lunch is to be served. Estimating quantities is the most daunting task for beginners, so here is a helpful handy guide passed down to me by my great-aunt Eileen McWilson (not from the McScrooge branch of the family, as you will see).

These ingredients will be sufficient for a family of four, so adjust accordingly where necessary. On 29 December it will be necessary to throw out all the uneaten items that have not already gone off. Christmas pudding and Christmas cake will both survive until the third millennium without special care; simply leave on an open cupboard shelf to mature.

My own purchases for Christmas are more modest, and consist of a packet of Mr Kipling's assorted mince-pies, the cost of which I share with a neighbour. I do, nevertheless, enjoy a nice turkey or other roasted and stuffed game bird. How I recall a Christmas past when two friends insisted on serving a roast goose. My juices began to run at about 6 p.m., when we were allowed a gin and tonic. By

AUNTIE EILEEN'S
CHRISTMAS NECESSITIES

BAKING

16 FAMILY SIZED PORK PIES

11 5LB CHRISTMAS PUDDINGS

5 CHRISTMAS CAKES

5,682 MINCE-PIES

3,126 ASSORTED JAM AND LEMON CURD TARTS*

GROCERIES

2CWT BRUSSELS SPROUTS

15CWT POTATOES (MASHING)

6CWT POTATOES (ROASTING)

20LB CHIPOLATAS

20LB SAUSAGEMEAT

10LB SAGE & ONION STUFFING

1 STONE CHESTNUTS

13 LARGE TERRINES OR PATES

15 WHITE SLICED LOAVES

6 FRENCH LOAVES

14 BOXES AFTER EIGHTS

17 SACKS TANGERINES (WITH PIPS)

*(WHENEVER MY FATHER WANTED TWO OF THESE,
HE SHOUTED FOR A LEMON TURD!)

9 p.m., nothing had reached the table and not a single further drink had been served. We finally carved that bird at around midnight. Since then, of course, I have learned that this is part of the tradition of Christmas lunch, which must never be hurried. I know that some of you will have slavishly followed Delia Smith's kitchen countdown over the years, but please allow me to simplify your life by offering you this foolproof guide to the perfect traditional Christmas Day meal.

21 December

The Ultimate Sprout Recipe

The first pan to bring to the boil is the one containing the water for the Brussels sprouts. These should be peeled and given a cross underneath to signify Easter. This also helps them to cook more quickly, which is invaluable. Once they come to the boil, keep an eye on the pan, and replenish with water when this becomes too low. After about three days of rapid boiling with the lid off, they should almost be cooked. You'll know they're done when they're bright yellow in colour and have taken on the pungent aroma of old people. Add copious amounts of salt to taste. For an extra-luxurious dish, do not place a knob of butter on top, use lard instead.

22 December

While the sprouts are boiling, begin peeling potatoes for your 'roasties'. If you start scraping and taking out the eyes today, these should be ready to put in the roasting pan on Boxing Day, which will make a nice change from having roast potatoes with your Christmas lunch.

You should now put the pudding on. The best way to cook this is to stand it on the kitchen table, then boil a huge pan of water until it steams the entire house out for three days. This is the absolute minimum steaming time for traditional purposes, though even a 5lb pudding would have cooked in the microwave in about four minutes. When ready to serve, decorate with holly and cover with meths, which lights much more easily than brandy, and is a darned sight less expensive. The holly will crackle nicely when it catches fire and burns to a charred crisp.

23 December

Start defrosting the turkey. After forty-eight hours, you should just be able to prise open the larger of the two holes in the ends, and by inserting your arm up to the elbow, you will be able to feel a plastic bag. This will tear as you try to pull it towards you, so wait another twelve hours before trying to remove it a second time. When you eventually manage to get it out of the cavity, throw it immediately in the rubbish. It seems to contain nothing but unspeakably foul parts of fowl.

Amusing Things to Do

BETWEEN COURSES OF

Christmas Lunch

Entrée

MAKE BINOCULARS FROM CRACKER INNERS

PLAY 'KNUCKLES' WITH ANY DELICATE CHILDREN

STEP AEROBICS

Main Course

NIP INTO THE KITCHEN AND HAVE A POT NOODLE TO
STAVE OFF HUNGER PANGS

DECIDE ON A NAME FOR THE TURKEY

PINCH GRANDPA AND ALLOW A SMALL BOY TO TAKE THE BLAME

Dessert

BREAK WIND, THEN BEAT THE DOG

OPEN A SECOND BOTTLE OF LIEBFRAUMILCH AND HANG THE EXPENSE

WATCH GRANNY FINISH CHEWING

Followed by . . .

LEAVE THE DISHES TO SOAK (FOR TWO DAYS)

When it is thoroughly defrosted, you may start to roast the turkey in a very low oven for about a week. During this time, it is useful to set your alarm every two hours, especially during the night, so that you can check progress. After about fourteen hours, it will be done to a crisp on the outside and raw inside. This is how most families like it, but I do prefer a further three days to make sure it carves easily.

25 December

Gravy can be made the same day as lunch. You will need to make it about five times, as the first four attempts will be too lumpy. Eventually, you may prefer instant granules, which produce a sauce indistinguishable from gravy made with scalding-hot fat. When I run into acute problems in this area, I have occasionally overheard my more boisterous guests giggling and muttering something about 'one foot in the gravy', though I can't think why this should amuse them. Some years, I have even resorted to asking Delia to pop round and help out with this bit, which she's only too willing to do, as she herself prepares Christmas lunch on a quiet Sunday afternoon some time in August, then she wraps it in clingfilm, and just warms it through on the day, so she tells me. What a terrific woman!

When everything is ready to serve, make sure you have sharpened the carving knife properly, in order to be able to serve paper-thin slices of breast. Investing in a knife-sharpener will not be a false economy at this time of year, believe me. For the true home economist, used surgical implements can nowadays be obtained at knock-down prices thanks to multiple hospital closures up and down the country. A quick rinse before use in cold water will ensure no traces of blood from past amputations linger on the blade. Then, attack each bone of the bird individually with the scalpel blade, removing all flesh and sinew with a pair of tweezers.

For those who prefer a less traditional platter than 'turkey and trimmings', here are some more innovative suggestions.

As you lead your guests to the groaning table, remark that – as you are an avid follower of food fashions, though definitely not a 'foodie' – you have it on good authority that 'nouvelle cuisine' is making a comeback. Mention in passing that you've had a sneak preview of the publisher's draft of Delia's new collection, and she predicts that 'Small is going to be HUGE', if you see what I mean. In this manner, you will be perfectly justified in proudly presenting your famished guests with lunch *à la Scrooge*: mangetout and baby sweetcorn, lovingly arranged on a bed of puréed cranberry sauce, to reflect the traditional green, red and gold colours of Christmas, naturally!

If that sounds like too much trouble, then one could espouse the joys of 'cuisine Provençale', and go on to re-create the flavours of rustic peasant dishes with a medley of cabbage and a delicate sprinkling of 'haricots baked' (vintage Heinz). If any voices dare to be raised in dissent, you simply retort by confidently claiming that they would have got Pacific Rim Cordon Bleu, but for the fact that (a) you've recently joined the League Against Kangaroo Culling, and (b) you've heard that many people have an allergy to coriander.

For those of you who really want to push the boat out in a more 'alternative' way, and still ensure your guests flee before you reach the main course, then why not as they arrive alert them all to the fact that you were converted to vegetarianism just three days ago, but that Ursula Ferrigno of the Vegetarian Society was kind enough to supply you with this wonderful recipe to replace turkey. It's a savoury delight which she calls 'Luxury Nut and Seed Loaf with Cranberry, Apple and Brandy Sauce'. Just show them the following recipe, and I suspect the very first ingredient will provoke a stampede for the front door, with several departing guests whimpering things like 'butterball' and 'parson's nose'.

Luxury Nut and Seed Loaf with Cranberry, Apple and Brandy Sauce

225g bulgar wheat	110g sunflower seeds
330ml boiling water	110g poppy seeds
3 x 15ml spoons soya sauce	250g onion, finely chopped
175g pistachio nuts	4 x 15ml spoons fresh and finely chopped parsley
175g pine nuts	2 x 15ml spoons dried thyme
225g blanched almonds	4 large free-range eggs, lightly whisked
175g cashew nuts	4 x 15ml spoons olive oil
110g hazelnuts	a little oil for pouring on roast

1 Place wheat in a mixing bowl and pour on the boiling water and soya sauce. Cover and let swell for 25 minutes. Grind nuts and seeds to a medium-fine consistency. Mix together with the wheat. Stir in the onion, parsley, thyme, eggs and oil. Mix well and allow to stand.

2 Oil a large baking sheet and line with greaseproof paper. Form a loaf with the nut mixture in the shape of a real, succulent piece of meat, about 10cm wide, press firmly together and prick the top with a fork. Pour on a little oil and sprinkle with some extra nuts (optional) and cap loosely with a foil hood. Bake in oven 190°C/375°F/Gas Mark 5 for 40 minutes.

3 Take off hood (not yours, silly, the one on the roast), baste with oil on baking sheet and continue to bake for a further 10 minutes. Place in a large serving dish, then cool, easing off the paper as you do so. Cover with the hood until ready to garnish.

4 Carve in the style of your favourite turkey.

My word, Ursula, that sounds delicious! If this sort of thing catches on, and in my book it's bound to, then I foresee bankruptcy for poor old Bernard Matthews.

Another ploy, which works especially well when there are children around, is to bring in two pet rabbits from the hutch down at the bottom of the garden, and to let the kiddies play with the lovely fluffy bunnies on the carpet for half an hour or so. Then look at your watch, get up from your armchair and say: 'Well, I'd better put the oven on. Now, which of those two do you fancy for lunch?' If there aren't tears and squeals within seconds, then my middle name isn't Ebenezer.

Sometimes, children insist on having their own 'special' meal. On these occasions, I prepare them something absolutely scrummy like jelly made out of Night Nurse – keeps them quiet for hours afterwards.

None of the above tactics may have worked to your total satisfaction: in other words, by the time lunch is ready, you might have a few people who relish the thought of freshly slaughtered bunny giblet gravy or dried nut toast. To those of you in this predicament, I can offer but one further hint … an age-old ploy, silly maybe, childish I grant you, but still a trusted trick in my opinion. After saying grace, with the lavishly prepared platters steaming away in front of each person, make sure everyone has been served and that not a scrap remains on the serving-dishes before passing the salt to your least favourite male freeloader and the pepper to your least favourite female. From both of these receptacles, you will have unscrewed the cap to the point where, as soon as they begin to shake the cruet, their dinners are drenched in condiment and unfit to eat. And, oh dear, there's nothing left to give them, and everyone has started to tuck in. They'll be off home at the trot to see what's lurking down at the bottom of the deep-freeze.

While serving your vegetarian friends, point out sympathetically that you have made sure that all the ingredients you have used are guaranteed 'veggie'. Then casually add: 'I mean ... suet *is* vegetarian, isn't it?' Or accidentally on purpose pass the gravy boat across their plate and allow a few drops of rare meat juice to dribble on to their nut cutlets. Immediately rush to the kitchen, and return with feeble apologies about having a couple of eggs left if they'd prefer a plain omelette.

If you still have a few cling-on stragglers who refuse to depart until you've served them some form of pudding, then offer these gluttons a simple, home-made trifle. I usually 'pass' on this particular dish, claiming that since my schooldays I have had no fondness for cold custard. However, the reason has much more to do with a story I like to tell while dishing up gargantuan portions to my guests. It concerns the late Arthur Askey, Tommy Trinder and a couple of other variety artistes who were staying in rather dreary digs in Macclesfield one pantomime season. The landlady was particularly niggardly, having stuck signs everywhere reminding guests not to attempt to smuggle young chorus girls into the bedrooms, and to avoid depositing 'solids' in the upstairs loo. Each night, the chaps would return home late from the theatre, desperately in need of alcoholic refreshment. Once they had located her hidden supply of sherry, they helped themselves to a nightly tot of finest Emva Cream. By the third night, it dawned on them that the level was rapidly dwindling, and that they had better think about replacing it. Arthur had a much finer idea, and took the bottle off to the 'smallest room' where he replenished it with amber liquid from his own supply, if you see what I mean.

By the Sunday, the landlady had rather mollified, and had quite taken to the mischievous foursome. So, in honour of their departure for Hull that same evening, she prepared a terrific tea, at the end of which the comics complimented

her kindness, saying they had especially enjoyed her home-made trifle. 'Oh, I'm so glad you liked it,' said the beaming dragoness, 'because, as it was a special occasion, I decided to put in extra sherry!'

The very last hangers-on will by now expect some after-dinner friandise, such as chocolates and coffee. This is where Black Magic will come in handy for the first time in your life. There is not – and correct me if I'm wrong here – a single household in the British Isles that doesn't have, somewhere within its four walls, a half-started box of this vile confectionery that nobody had the stomach to finish. Furthermore, there on the bottom layer you will find at least two coffee creams (and probably a bitter orange). Thus, you can satisfy any guest's desire for coffee and chocolate in one simple mouthful. Delicious.

Finally, at this point you may wish to offer liqueurs, which is an excellent way to dispose of unwanted dregs at the bottom of bottles such as Tia Maria, Kahlua, Malibu, Baileys, etc.

In the event of real emergency – for instance, when an overnight stay is suggested – immediately assume a comatose position in front of the television where you must remain oblivious even to the loud hum at the end of broadcasting. You may rise from your most comfortable armchair only when you hear the front door being gently closed behind the last of the impertinent intruders as they depart into the chill night air.

You will soon experience a most satisfying feeling of well-being.

DRINK

D o not be rash! Do not go mad! There is *nothing* wrong, in these days of breathalysers, alcoholism and health fads, in presenting all your guests with a simple fruit cup – I usually go for a blend of long-life orange juice, a dash of Ribena and a can of pineapple chunks (using every last drop of the liquor). For those of you who will insist on spoiling a beautiful cocktail with valuable proof spirit, then may I recommend the addition of small quantities of Listerine or very cheap gin (best purchased in a Calais hypermarket). Alternatively, use up the remains of old bottles of advocaat, Blue Bols, Benylin (super-strength only) or Night Nurse.

While most of the elements of a family Christmas are left to the discretion of the host, there is actually ancient legislation that says you must serve mulled wine … even though few people can stomach more than one plastic cupful in the course of a year. Apart from scalding the mouth, it always seems to contain unidentifiable pieces of brown fruit with unpleasant textures. So, whereas throughout this invaluable book I have presented an 'anti-traditional' approach, I cannot be seen to be encouraging lawlessness. Here, then, is a straightforward guide to mulled wine which, while maintaining the spirit of my thesis, should also keep the authorities off your back.

My Traditional Mulled Wine
INGREDIENTS

1 litre of random red wine – I am reluctant to recommend a particular variety, but remember, you are NOT trying to spoil anyone. Go for something with a screw top, or better still something shipped in polythene with a name that sounds vaguely East European.

2 litres of water – there is nothing remotely amusing to be said about water (unless you live in the Thames area, in which case, good luck!).

1 orange stuck with cloves —
I'm assuming this means cloves
of garlic.

Miscellaneous fruit — oranges,
lemons, tomatoes, whatever.

4 tablespoons of sugar — or
equivalent of Hermesetas.

A small liquorice stick, a slightly
larger cinnamon stick and the
thumping great stick you use to
play 'fetch' with Fido.

2 teaspoons of fresh or ground
ginger or medium-sized slice of
McVitie's ginger cake.

A generous splash of your favourite
liqueur — Crème de Menthe would
be ideal. Be aware that Cointreau
provides too 'sympathetic' a flavour
for your needs.

INSTRUCTIONS

1 Throw all the ingredients into a
cauldron. Boil like mad for about an
hour, stirring occasionally if you're
already in the vicinity.

2 There is no 2. See, I said it
was simple.

PLEASE NOTE

If you are concerned about boiling away the alcohol, you might like to serve with a chaser of mouthwash, since little else will register with your guests' scorched tastebuds. This will help loosen things up, encourage your visitors to get any slight niggles off their chest, and you are likely to witness Cousin Frances (the fifty-year-old spinster) trying to 'limbo' under the dining table.

There is one effective method of hiding the fact that you are not willing to stump up hard-earned sovereigns for party beverages that, a day later, could be relabelled 'World's Most Expensive Urine'. Simply spend a casual hour or two hanging around the local recycling bank, offering helpfully to dispose of the aluminium cans and glass bottles for the environmentally conscious people who arrive in their huge estate cars and four-wheel drives. Usually, their refuse will be neatly packed in cardboard boxes or carrier-bags, making your task much cleaner. You might also like to offer them the chance to empty their car ashtrays, which they would probably have done on the pavement anyway, if you hadn't been standing there. Once the depositors have left, make for home with their empties. Scatter these all around the living room and kitchen, placing most of the dog-ends in the rubber plant for that authentic party look. When guests arrive later in the day, make profuse and abject apologies, explaining that Gazza, Oliver Reed and Princess Margaret came round uninvited to wish you the compliments of the season … and now look at the place!

> **PROOF OF THE PUDDING**
>
> **THE ASHES** of a long-lost uncle were accidently mixed in a Christmas pudding after being sent to his family. "The pud tasted wonderful," sobbed one upset relative in Taranto, Italy.
>
> Daily Star 04/01/97

An essential part of any gathering where drinks are being offered is the ritual of the cocktail nibbles — which has nothing to do with foreplay! Any aspiring Scrooge will have noticed that these pre-dinner crispy things are seldom touched in polite society, thus presenting the host with the chance to save a few precious pennies. For instance, instead of filling a bowl with Twiglets, just use twigs. And instead of laying out KP Skips, why not experiment with those little shavings of polystyrene that you found in the box your new toaster came in? These also come in peanut shapes and in imitation cucumber slices, which are extremely convincing. Nobody who eats one will know the difference, or if they do, they'll be too well mannered to make any mention of it.

A word of warning: at about this time of year, there is an unusual furry creature which, though normally dormant for fifty-one weeks, comes slowly out of hibernation at the seasonal sound of a bottle of Babycham being opened. The Latin name for this shy animal is *Greatus Auntus*, commonly known as the Old Moo. On emerging from her nephew's car, she will proceed directly to your own favourite armchair and remain immobile until your television breaks down or the bingo hall reopens. Amazingly, she will renounce her vow of teetotalism exclusively for your benefit, and expect to be attached to a drip-feed of sweet sherry or port and lemon for thirty-six hours. It might be worth spiking the drink with a spoonful of liquid senna pod early in the day, so that she occupies a throne in another part of the house, preferably out of earshot. Alternatively, tell her you have found a new drink which will be much more to her liking, then pour a large glass of Underborg served at just above room temperature. If you take this option, however, make sure you have a supply of kitchen towel and a large bowl to hand.

On occasion, I have resorted to a theatrical manoeuvre to dissuade my guests from asking for anything stronger than a soft drink. This involves some preparation, and works best as a long, rambling anecdote about your old friend 'Johnny Stage-Thespian' (any larger-than-life recently deceased actor will do). With a tear welling in your eye, slowly explain how you saw him only hours before his last curtain fell, as he was in intensive care following three failed liver transplants and a kidney operation. If this doesn't slow down their consumption, say that at the express request of his widow, you have removed all booze from the house until after his memorial service, around Easter.

Indeed, some of my disciples have even been known to bring forward Lent, and abstain from booze for six weeks around Christmas-time, in case they don't make it to Ash Wednesday. This has always struck me as a little implausible, and rather on a par with trying to convince your nearest and dearest that you have become a Muslim. While it is easy for the ladies simply to pretend they have taken the veil, the gentlemen using this far-fetched excuse may feel a little queasy if they have to explain their plans for an imminent circumcision …

TAKE IT LIKE A MAN
by Boy George

I spent Christmas Day at my parents in Shooters Hill, no heroin, no cold turkey. I used painkillers to stabilise myself, and a bit of spliff smoked quietly in the toilet.

Boxing Day evening I threw a party at my house in Hampstead for a bunch of the most mismatched guests ever. Mum, Dad, my brothers and sister, Auntie Heather and Uncle Jim, and most of London's users and abusers. Mum and Dad were now fully aware of my new habits. They surveyed the assembled company for someone to blame. There was no way they could have suspected Ginty who turned up all mumsie with two kids and her ex-husband. I was off my head, running around with a video camera. Mum cornered me. 'What have you taken? It ain't just drink.' Without actually saying, she blamed Marilyn. He felt her disapproving glare burn through him.

The party fizzled out around five, a few of us went back to St John's Wood and carried on. The two Richards, Hippie and Habit, Warren, Tranny, Fat Tony and my brother Kevin. We finished off. the morning with a trip to London Zoo. We looked wilder than any of the animals. Tony tried to stick a long-eared ginger bunny up his jumper. He soon put it back when it bit him. I argued with a waiter in the canteen because he wouldn't serve us beer. 'Only coffee, tea or soft drinks, sir.'

DRUGS

Let's be honest about this, most of us require some form of drugs to get us through this stressful time of year. Wherever your favourite supply, whoever your favourite supplier, contact them early and place your order well in advance, as they will be hard pushed to satisfy all demand. They will also expect immediate payment, preferably in cash. Don't be surprised if you find it more difficult than usual to obtain exactly what you want in the quantities you had hoped for. The point is, to make sure you have an adequate 'stash' of *something*, to keep you going until the dealers are ready to do business again … which could well be some time after 2 January in remoter areas of the country. Buy much larger quantities than usual for added value, and for peace of mind. The selection should include something to take you up, something to take you down and plenty to bring you round the following day. My recommended list includes: Setlers, Paracetamol, Pepto-Bismol, Alka Seltzer, Resolve and, of course, Prozac.

The morning after

If none of the above has soothed your aching brow, then try either of the age-old remedies printed alongside.

It might be worth pointing out at this juncture that certain important preparations could be made to prevent a bottle-neck at the bathroom between the hours of 8 a.m. and 12 noon on the day following your party. Embarrassment and disputes can be avoided by placing a row of chairs outside the bathroom and lavatory doors, so that an orderly queue is formed.
If the wait threatens to be prolonged, those in line might appreciate the occasional Alton Towers-style notice informing them that from this point in the queue there will be a forty-five-minute wait, and so on.

Into a large tumbler pour a tot of whisky, a tot of ginger wine, a tot of tequila, a dash of Angostura bitters, a measure of vermouth, fresh tomato juice, tonic water, and top up to the rim with cold tea. The result will be partial oblivion … well, after all, you couldn't feel any worse.

The Prairie Oyster is a traditional cure for hangovers, and consists of a dozen raw egg yolks, a dash of Worcestershire sauce, a teaspoon of salt, a generous pinch of curry powder and half a pint of port. Without mixing the ingredients, swallow down in one gulp. Make sure you are within firing range of the toilet bowl, as you will throw up immediately and feel instantly better for the experience.

GUESTS

I t is especially lovely to be surrounded by your close friends at this season, particularly when they arrive bearing copious amounts of food and drink ... as they so seldom do. Generally, when I see folk heading up the garden path with not even a Party Seven between them, I fling wide the door and with my broadest smile I shout down to the gate, 'It's all right. I've just phoned the off-licence and they're open for another half-hour. See you in a bit.' Then firmly slam the door, in case they didn't quite get the message.

They'll return before long, accompanied by the lovely traditional sound of chinking bottles. Once inside, they will assume you have nothing more pressing to do than devote your entire evening to entertaining them, so I often like to kick off proceedings by initiating a bit of a topical debate, which can become rather wonderfully heated. For example, you make sure you have at least one master of foxhounds and one member of the League Against Cruel Sports, then say something like: 'I hear Tolpuddle Council is threatening to ban sportsmen from skinning live hamsters on all municipal land.' Just wait about three seconds before you start to see some real fur fly, during which time you can retire to your study with a favourite book, or go upstairs to watch *The Sound of Music* on the bedroom TV.

Another universally liked subject is politics. Start by insisting that Mussolini could have sorted out the crisis on the railways here in no time. If this is slow to get off the ground, suggest that Hitler may have had something after all.

Or that old stand-by — royalty. You must first request that everyone be seated quietly for the start of the Queen's Speech (though do please make sure they are all upstanding for the National Anthem). Just see what happens when you suddenly leap up halfway through the section about the Royal Yacht cruising up the Limpopo, slam the off-button, and complain loudly that we got the same bloody speech and the same bloody lemon cardigan last year.

Then, who can forget religion at a time like this? There's nothing to compare

CHRISTMAS DAY PLAYLIST
Tracks to Make the Party Go with a Swing

'Christmas Will Be
Just Another Lonely Day' . . . . Brenda Lee
'Dragging Me Down' . . . . Inspiral Carpets
'I Want to Be Alone' 2wo Third3
'Everyday Is Like Sunday' . . . . Morrissey
'Cryin'' . . . . Roy Orbison
'The Desperate Hours' . . . . Marc Almond
'No Christmas' . . . . Wedding Present
'No More (I Can't Stand It)' . . . . Maxx
'Pain' . . . . Betty Wright
'There Goes My Everything' . . . . Elvis Presley
'Take It or Leave It' . . . . The Searchers
'What More Do You Want' . . . . Frankie Vaughan
'Money Money Money' . . . . Abba
'It's Over' . . . . Roy Orbison
'It Seems to Hang On' . . . . Ashford & Simpson
'A Bad Night' . . . . Cat Stevens
'What Kind of Fool Am I?' . . . . Anthony Newley
'You Can Have It All' . . . . George McCrae
'The Wisdom of a Fool' . . . . Ronnie Carroll
'I (Who Have Nothing)' . . . . Shirley Bassey
'I Wanna Stay Home' . . . . Jellyfish
'Christmas in Dreadland' . . . . Judge Dread
'Eve of Destruction' . . . . Barry McGuire
'Heartbreak Hotel' . . . . Elvis Presley
'Is It Really Over?' . . . . Jim Reeves

with a blazing row between a few warring factions on Jesus Christ's birthday, of all days. Well, when better, if you ask me!! Start things off tentatively with an immaculately conceived: 'Well, that Joseph was a mug, considering the Child Support Agency would never have believed his wife's far-fetched story!' The apocalypse should have abated some time around mid-February. Alternatively, to avoid disturbing the neighbours with too much shouting, you could try boring everyone out of the house by suggesting a debate around the table on proportional representation, or asking everyone who they think has been the most effectual Archbishop of Canterbury over the past thirty years.

When your guests seriously threaten to outstay their welcome, and assuming the weather is particularly bitter, the simplest remedy is to turn off the central heating, and start pretending to phone a plumber, wailing that your boiler has burst on Christmas Day! For additional effect, don a balaclava, three pullovers and mittens. An overcoat may be taking things a little too far. Or offer to put on your new CD of Russ Abbott singing favourite Christmas carols, with Max Bygraves's wartime hits to follow.

Better still, begin to entertain anyone who's still awake with stories of your recent prostate operation, and the double hernia complications. You could always offer to show them your collection of vintage trusses, or steer the conversation towards the benefits of colonic irrigation with particular reference to a seasonal diet of sprouts! Works every time!!

From time to time over the so-called 'festive season', the doorbell will ring, heralding the arrival of countless more unwanted 'guests'. Show them in, by all means, but I have learned from long experience that a flair for make-up, wigs and cross-dressing can be a boon at such moments. Gentlemen should answer the door in full drag and complete make-up, insisting that they must be addressed as 'Cheryl', loudly announcing to the whole street that this has been their private residence since 1976, that the 'floor show' begins in twenty minutes, and that they should have their luncheon vouchers ready for inspection, 'same as last week, big boy'. This final remark generally has an immediately subduing effect on any wives present, though I am unsure quite why.

MERRY CHRISTMAS

by E. B. White

From this high midtown hall, undecked with boughs, unfortified with mistletoe, we send forth our tinselled greetings as of old, to friends, to readers, to strangers of many conditions in many places. Merry Christmas to uncertified accountants, to tellers who have made a mistake in addition, to girls who have made a mistake in judgment, to grounded airline passengers, and to all those who can't eat clams! We greet with particular warmth people who wake and smell smoke. To captains of river boats in snowy mornings we send an answering toot at this holiday time. Merry Christmas to intellectuals and other despised minorities! Merry Christmas to the musicians of Muzak and men whose shoes don't fit. Greetings of the season to unemployed actors and the blacklisted everywhere who suffer for sins uncommitted; a holly thorn in the thumb of compilers of lists! Greetings to wives who can't find their glasses and to poets who can't find their rhymes! Merry Christmas to the unloved, the misunderstood, the overweight. Joy to the authors of books whose titles begin with the word 'How' (as though they knew!). Greetings to people with a ringing in their ears; greetings to growers of gourds, to shearers of sheep, and to makers of change in the lonely underground booths! Merry Christmas to old men asleep in libraries! Merry Christmas to people who can't stay in the same room with a cat! We greet, too, the boarders in boarding-houses on 25th December, the duennas in Central Park in fair weather and foul, and young lovers who got nothing in the mail. Merry Christmas to people who plant trees in city streets; merry Christmas to people who save prairie chickens from extinction! Greetings of a purely mechanical sort to machines that think – plus a sprig of artificial holly. Joyous Yule to Cadillac owners whose conduct is unworthy of their car! Merry Christmas to the defeated, the forgotten, the inept; joy to all dandiprats and bunglers! We send, most particularly and most hopefully, our greetings and our prayers to soldiers and guardsmen on land and sea and in the air – the young men doing the hardest things at the hardest time of their life. To all such, Merry Christmas, blessings, and good luck! We greet the Secretaries-designate, the President-elect; Merry Christmas to our new leaders, peace on earth, good will, and good management! Merry Christmas to couples unhappy in doorways! Merry Christmas to all who think they are in love but aren't sure! Greetings to people waiting for trains that will take them in the wrong direction, to people doing up a bundle and the string is too short, to children with sleds and no snow! We greet ministers who can't think of a moral, gagmen who can't think of a joke. Greetings, too, to the inhabitants of other planets: see you soon! And last, we greet all skaters on small natural ponds at the edge of woods toward the end of afternoon. Merry Christmas, skaters! Ring, steel! Grow red, sky! Die down, wind! Merry Christmas to all and to all a good morrow!

GAMES

I think we've all had quite enough of *Baby Boomer, Trivial Pursuit, Dingbats, Jenga* and *Pictionary* to last us a good few Christmases to come, so here are my suggestions for some novel Xmas pastimes and ways to while away the leaden hours between about 4 p.m. and 8 p.m., before the pork pies and Christmas cake are brought out – assuming, of course, that someone else is spending those four hours doing the washing up, not yourself.

My first rule for a truly painful sequence of games is to hide the telly for the day, thus preventing anyone from 'opting out' and saying that they absolutely must catch the seventy-third screening of *The Wizard of Oz* or that they don't want this to be the first year of their life in which they miss Rolf Harris presenting Christmas Disneytime. Once that is safely secured out of sight, you are free to announce that in fifteen minutes' time, at your invitation, there will be a visit from the local amateur operatic society. You can't expect a full complement, of course, as some will have prior commitments, but anticipate at least thirty-eight large-bosomed ladies scented of pear-drops and a dozen balding men in bifocals to be on the doorstep at the allotted hour. Suggest to your guests that the 'thesps' would be more than happy to perform a selection of Wagner's greatest hits around the upright for the next seventeen hours (unfortunately, a heavily condensed version of his epic entertainments), and then possibly lighten the tone a little as darkness sets in, with perhaps highlights of Gilbert and Sullivan to a piano-accordion accompaniment. There's nothing to beat classy performances of this calibre. One so rarely has the opportunity to partake of real live theatre these days.

For those who prefer something more subtle – and, dare I say, more seasonal – why not have over the local amateur dramatic society, who may be able to spare a couple of hours to re-enact the Nativity. Better still, combine the two and create a vaudevillian revue with a Christmas slant. If any visitors are still awake, then encourage them to join in the fun by allocating non-speaking roles such as shepherds, livestock, etc.

If all the above strike you as a little too noisy, then I have another delightful entertainment which could leave your guests comatose in a matter of minutes. First, you must bring forth from the understairs cupboard your entire year's store of back copies of *Hello!* magazine – all fifty-two of them. Spread them around the floor, and provide each person with a pair of scissors. Everyone is given the task of cutting out pictures of certain celebrities which will then be transformed into a beautiful Nativity collage. At the end of the evening, this frieze can either be hung around the room in the style of the Bayeux Tapestry, or, more generously, divided up into sections, and presented to everyone who was there, as a memento of a beautiful moment.

The possibilities for deciding which celebrity best suits which role are endless, though I have a few suggestions to set you off in the right direction:

THE PERFORMERS

JANE ASHER ....*Mary*
ELTON JOHN ....*Mary's sister*
LILY SAVAGE ....*The Midwife*
PAUL GASCOIGNE ....*The Innkeeper*
THE DUCHESS OF YORK ....*The Innkeeper's wife*
DONALD SINDEN ⎫
EDWARD FOX ⎬..................*The Magi*
ROBERT HARDY ⎭
CHRIS EVANS ⎫
DANNY BAKER ⎬..................*Shepherds*
DAMIEN HIRST ⎭
JEREMY PAXMAN ....*Joseph*
LEONARDO DI CAPRIO ....*The Angel Gabriel*
MICHAEL JACKSON ....*Baby Jesus*
CAMILLA PARKER-BOWLES ....*The donkey*

Granted the three Magi may be a little pale-skinned for real authenticity, but think how magnificent they'd look astride camels ... There will be no end of helpful suggestions for substitutes, so be prepared to dismiss these as the crude jokes

they blatantly are. For instance, someone will suggest that the Angel Gabriel should be Melinda Messenger, which is not a very clever pun on her name. Another wag will doubtless ask why she cannot be the Virgin Mary, to which there is no decent answer. Doubtless, too, someone will see a picture of the former pop sensations the Spice Girls, who were associated with many adjectives, including Sporty Spice, Scary Spice, Sweet Spice, Posh Spice and Ginger Spice. Somehow Virgin Spice fails to have any ring of truth to it. Take it from me, at Christmas-time the only authentic version of this name game is Old Spice. Jeremy Paxman is the only possible candidate for Joseph. While on the road to Bethlehem, he could use his University Challenge encouragements to Mary, telling her, 'Come on. Oh, do hurry up.' Otherwise, perhaps Michael Jackson should be recast as Joseph, since both their wives may have practised immaculate conception.

When the party threatens to sag a little – as even the best parties unaccountably do – you might like to try this little game to warm things up a bit. It's called Snap Dragon and was immensely popular in England during the 1800s, which is surprising really, considering they had neither running water nor a reliable fire brigade in those days. First, you need to half fill a large bowl with brandy – though I'm sure meths or white spirit would do as well, at a fraction of the cost – and light it. Then throw a handful of raisins or sultanas into the flames. The party guests must now take turns snatching the flaming raisins and popping them into their mouths. The flames do go out as soon as the mouth shuts, so speed and dexterity are essential! However, I do not recommend this game to anyone with artificial eyelashes or a tendency to wear copious amounts of hair lacquer. So, if Dusty Springfield or Baroness Thatcher has turned up at your house, you'll have to ask them respectfully just to sit this one out with a glass of stout.

In similarly old-fashioned vein, try a game of hide-and-seek. Count to ten as everybody else finds somewhere to hide. Then, settle down in your favourite chair and watch the telly in peace for at least twenty minutes while they all ponder whether they're the last ones to be found or the first ones to leap from their hiding-place. Or, if you yourself are looking for a hiding-place, always go straight to the lavatory with a good magazine. Again, you will have a brief respite until someone starts hammering the door down in desperate cramps. Finally,

CHRISTMAS MOVIES

Film	Comments	Rating
The Dark Night of the Soul	Or anything by Ingmar Bergman	★★★★★
Schindler's List	Guaranteed to ruin even the happiest of Christmas days	★★★★
The Gospel According to St Matthew	A bit like starting the joke with the punchline	★★★
Reservoir Dogs	Helps emphasise the fate that befalls many Christmas pets	★★
Trainspotting	Just to shock the old folk who have woken up in front of the telly	★

there's that other party classic called Truth or Dare. I have never quite understood why people tell the truth in this game. Why not lie? I know I always do ...

Which also reminds me of Six Degrees of Separation – a game that can be played in two versions, fact or fantasy. First, start with an unlikely figure of fun from the celebrity circuit, let's say Cecil Parkinson, for instance. Next, a second celebrity is named, who must be linked to the noble lord through no more than six sets of partners. For example, you might say, Mick Jagger and Jerry Hall ... Jerry Hall and Jerry Hayes ... Jerry Hayes and Hayzee Fantayzee ... Hayzee Fantayzee and Cecil Parkinson. Which is obviously on the fantastical side, but then it is Christmas.

Once in a while, you should set yourself the task of organising a really good theme party for Christmas, on the lines of Vicars and Tarts or Black and White. Invite everyone you know, well in advance. My tried and tested combinations are these:

Jeffrey Archer and Cynthia Payne
Undertakers & mortuary attendants
Scoutmasters, choirboys and vicars
Naturist carol singers
Gyles Brandreth and Jilly Cooper

The turnout is unlikely to reach double figures, unless you number some extremely sick people among your friends, and you needn't get in much more than a six-pack of low-alcohol lager and some unsalted peanuts in their shells (since nobody ever touches these at parties).

It is not unusual at this time of year to welcome a small quantity of elderly party guests, who may be a little less energetic than the majority of us. And yet, you know, there's no reason why they shouldn't be a part of all the fun. One way in which I like to involve them is a little treat called the Oldies' Sweepstake. As with any sweepstake, there are a number of winning possibilities, which each person in the room gambles on. The idea is to put one penny into the kitty in exchange for a slip of paper. On the slip of paper is written a possible scenario featuring one of the elderly relatives doing something typically endearing at this time of year.

Recommended Reading

Light relief when Christmas gets too much

Selected by R. Wilson

Heart of Darkness
by Joseph Conrad

The Anatomy of Melancholy
by Robert Burton

Cancer Ward
by Alexander Solzhenitsyn

Hard Times
by Charles Dickens

The Inferno
by Dante Alighieri

Desperate Remedies
by Thomas Hardy

Every Man Out of His Humour
by Ben Jonson

Bleak House
by Charles Dickens

Heartbreak House
by George Bernard Shaw

Long Day's Journey Into Night
by Eugene O'Neill

The Domesday Book
by Various

Thoughts on the Cause of the Present Discontents
by Edmund Burke

You will obviously want to modify the list to take account of the foibles of your own particular set of Gothics, but here are some suggestions:

- Gran recounts how in her day you had to go to school on Christmas Day.
- Gran recounts how in her day you had to go to school with no boots!
- Great-Uncle Len gets confused as the Queen's Speech on the wireless is not read by George VI.
- Grandpa puts on his smelly old slippers and pops the brand-new ones on to the flame-effect gas fire, causing toxic black smoke to billow down the street.
- Granny's teeth pop out under the mistletoe.
- Auntie Edie's hearing-aid packs up during a game of Chinese Whispers.
- Uncle Derek tells the story about eating maggots in the trenches in Egypt.

What happens next is that everyone settles back in a comfortable chair with a glass of brandy or whisky, and waits until one of the above happens. Whoever has the piece of paper featuring the correct scenario wins the entire kitty!! Alas, old folk being the predictable pain that they are, the game can sometimes be over in a very short space of time, in which case the kitty will have to be replenished, and the race rerun.

THE TWELVE DAYS OF CHRISTMAS

by Allen Sherman

ON THE FIRST DAY OF CHRISTMAS,
MY TRUE LOVE GAVE TO ME,
A JAPANESE TRANSISTOR RADIO.

ON THE SECOND DAY OF CHRISTMAS,
MY TRUE LOVE GAVE TO ME,
GREEN POLKA DOT PYJAMAS,
AND A JAPANESE TRANSISTOR RADIO.
(It's a Nakashuma.)

ON THE THIRD DAY OF CHRISTMAS,
MY TRUE LOVE GAVE TO ME,
A CALENDAR BOOK WITH THE NAME OF
MY INSURANCE MAN,
GREEN POLKA DOT PYJAMAS,
AND A JAPANESE TRANSISTOR RADIO.
(It's the Mark IV model. That's the one that's
discontinued.)

ON THE FOURTH DAY OF CHRISTMAS,
MY TRUE LOVE GAVE TO ME,
A SIMULATED ALLIGATOR WALLET,
A CALENDAR BOOK WITH THE NAME OF MY
    INSURANCE MAN,
GREEN POLKA DOT PYJAMAS,
AND A JAPANESE TRANSISTOR RADIO.
(And it comes in a leatherette case with holes in
it. So you could listen right through the case.)

ON THE FIFTH DAY OF CHRISTMAS,
MY TRUE LOVE GAVE TO ME,
A STATUE OF A LADY WITH A CLOCK WHERE
    HER STOMACH OUGHT TO BE,
A SIMULATED ALLIGATOR WALLET,
A CALENDAR BOOK WITH THE
    NAME OF MY INSURANCE MAN,
GREEN POLKA DOT PYJAMAS,
AND A JAPANESE TRANSISTOR RADIO.
(And it has a wire with a thing on one end that you
could stick in your ear, and a thing on the other end
that you can't stick anywhere because it's bent.)

ON THE SIXTH DAY OF CHRISTMAS,
MY TRUE LOVE GAVE TO ME,
A HAMMERED ALUMINIUM NUTCRACKER,
AND ALL THAT OTHER STUFF,
AND A JAPANESE TRANSISTOR RADIO.

CONTINUE UNTIL…

ON THE TWELFTH DAY OF CHRISTMAS,
ALTHOUGH IT MAY SEEM STRANGE,
ON THE TWELFTH DAY OF CHRISTMAS,
I'M GOING TO EXCHANGE:
AN AUTOMATIC VEGETABLE SLICER THAT WORKS
    WHEN YOU SEE IT ON TELEVISION BUT NOT
    WHEN YOU GET IT HOME,
A CHROMIUM COMBINATION MANICURE
    SCISSORS AND CIGARETTE LIGHTER,
A PAIR OF TEAKWOOD SHOWER CLOGS,
AN INDOOR PLASTIC BIRDBATH,
A PINK SATIN PILLOW THAT SAYS 'SAN DIEGO'
    WITH FRINGE ALL AROUND IT,
A HAMMERED ALUMINIUM NUTCRACKER,
A STATUE OF A LADY WITH A CLOCK WHERE
    HER STOMACH OUGHT TO BE,
A SIMULATED ALLIGATOR WALLET,
A CALENDAR BOOK WITH THE NAME OF MY
    INSURANCE MAN,
GREEN POLKA DOT PYJAMAS,
AND A JAPANESE TRANSISTOR RADIO.

FAMILY

Nobody ever invites family over for Christmas. Nobody ever needs to. Family always seems to invite itself and, what's more, family never takes no for an answer. You may as well accept this fact in mid-October: a large quantity of unwanted close family members plus assorted relatives looking like Ronald Reagan whom you haven't seen since there was last a family funeral will descend on you about nine weeks from now, and will have no hesitation about ruining Christmas for you. This is a simple fact of life.

For example, there on the doorstep will be Auntie Enid. No, she wasn't invited this year. You thought she'd passed away three months ago because you couldn't quite read the name on the card your brother sent you to say there was another cremation being stoked up. And, anyway, if that wasn't her funeral, you wouldn't have taken the morning off work. If this kind of vestigial twig of your family tree insists on dropping in (instead of dropping off!), then the best you can do is tell her she'll need to book a room in the nearest YWCA, because you've had the public health authorities round and there's a suspected outbreak of anthrax spores

It's a fair cop

By Wendy Holden

A POLICE sergeant who was one of the first arrested in a Christmas anti-drink-drive campaign was banned from driving for two years and fined £1,800.

Pamela De Neve crashed her car into a parked vehicle on December 4, less than five hours after the Suffolk Constabulary's Christmas anti-drink-driving campaign was launched. She admitted having had 12 glasses of wine.

Daily Telegraph 08/01/97

somewhere beneath the dining-room underlay. Explain to her as clearly as you can that it'll only be a twenty-pound cab fare each way to your house … no need to mention that it's double rate on Christmas Day, I think. When she protests that nobody wants her, suggest gently that she'd have a much better time staying in her sheltered accommodation with a visit from Meals on Wheels and some nice sugared almonds to keep her quiet, assuming these don't crack her spare set of dentures.

If your festive allergy symptoms are by this stage particularly acute, leaving you feeling that you cannot face even the *prospect* of another family Christmas, you might contemplate losing yourself altogether. Now, this could involve writing a dramatic 'Dear World' note and placing it under a fridge magnet (though it's unlikely anybody will spot it there for several days), or discarding a trail of clothing, as if abandoned, by the canal-side. In the most convincing cases, this could lead to much police activity, so do check the newspapers regularly and allay suspicions. Or you may consider something more prosaic, like hiring a cottage somewhere remote. This need not be expensive as, for many coastal resorts, Christmas is as 'off' as off-season gets.

The plan is to hide yourself away with a television, a video and a mountain of summer blockbusters to see you through until the middle of January. Alas, this too has certain drawbacks. Even if you are able to escape your *own* family, the minute you arrive at your hideout you will be besieged by a Swat team of local carol singers and well-meaning do-gooders, who will not rest (or at least will not give up knocking on the kitchen door) until you join them at the pub – where the landlord will wish to be known as 'mine host' – for the customary mulled wine, mince-pies and 'lock in'. On balance, it is safer to invite the family over to your place, where you will have a degree of control over proceedings. Well, I say 'invite' …

When Barbara rings – out of the blue two weeks before the 25th – to casually enquire if you were expecting her and cousin Norman round for lunch, then say extremely enthusiastically that, yes, there's absolutely no question, of course they are coming for turkey and all the trimmings. Wait about six seconds before adding the following: 'Do you know, by a strange coincidence, I ran into Norman's first wife recently, and felt it only polite to ask her and the boys over for a glass of something with us on the festive day. You don't mind, do you, Barbara?'

Many family members will assume, quite wrongly, that this is the ideal time to pay a visit accompanied by the children. The children? Unfortunately not *chez moi*. I have an incurable allergy to anything aged under-five (with the exception of a fine claret), and have developed a rare allergy which always strikes at the most inopportune moments … Christmas, Easter, birthdays, christenings, etc. The merest whiff of nappy rash may bring on a sudden attack, which could prove fatal. And nobody would want that on their conscience, surely. Maybe they could all go over to Cedric's. Not only is he 'single', he's a magician, too, and likes nothing better than performing in front of kids.

This is a robust stance, though one that is almost certainly doomed to failure. Kids there will be. And kids you must endure. By 10 a.m. on the day, I guarantee that your place will look as if someone has opened a crèche in the middle of war-torn Chechnya. And do not expect to be let off lightly merely because the children appear to have opened all their presents at home. Those gifts will constitute only a small fraction of their haul, and even before you've had time to quiz them within earshot of their parents about how long they'll be staying ('Don't you want to get home to play with your nuclear reactor set?'), their mother and father will be back outside unloading gaily coloured packages of not very well disguised shapes from the 'people carrier' which, incidentally, with half its seats folded can still hold seven body-builders and is, by your estimation, actually larger on the inside than on the outside, and in any case has a greater cubic capacity than your knock-through living room.

After about three hours, the

Christmas with in-laws turned into a real trial

BY PAUL WILKINSON

CHRISTMAS lunch with the in-laws can often be a trial, but for Scott Grogan it really did end up in front of a judge.

As a family squabble escalated into violence, the turkey finished on the floor amid the debris of a broken table, the dining-room door was wrenched from its hinges and Grogan's mother-in-law went screaming for help. Three policemen called to the scene were attacked by Grogan, 22, and finally arrested him after he threatened to kill his in-laws' entire family.

The Christmas from Hell started after Grogan had a row with his wife, Sarah Jane, when their four-week-old son, Connor, began to cry as lunch was being served at her family's home in Harrogate.

First he stormed out, but was persuaded to return, only to drink half a bottle of red wine in one swallow.

When his wife went to deal with her son's tears, said Jenny Kershaw, for the prosecution, "His fuse went and he caused pandemonium". He tried to grab the child but only succeeded in dropping him.

Then he head-butted his brother-in-law Simon Horne,

breaking his nose; pushed his wife and their son against a door so hard it snapped its hinges; tipped over the dining table, sending food and wine across the carpet; grabbed his father-in-law Robert Horne, a consulting engineer, by the throat and threw him into the Christmas tree entangling him in the lights; and drove his terrified mother-in-law, Audrey, out of the house.

Grogan, unemployed, from Tockwith, near York, told police that when he dropped the baby "things really started to go wrong". Mrs Kershaw added: "He may well be right".

John Devlin, for Grogan, who is unemployed, said it was a case of "Drink in, senses out". Grogan, who this week admitted at York Crown Court assaulting his brother-in-law, threatening to kill his family, and affray, was sentenced to 100 hours' community service.

He was also ordered to pay his brother and father-in-law £250 each as compensation for ruining their Christmas. After the case Mrs Grogan said: "Scott is so sorry for what he did."

The Times 28/5/97

CHRISTMAS TELLY

by Craig Brown

My own favourite is the 1973 Christmas *Top of the Pops* which I had been prevented from seeing in its entirety on its original showing. I was 16 at the time, and my family's 1973 Christmas lunch, like so many across the nation, was stricken by the knowledge that Christmas *Top of the Pops* was available in the next-door room. Should one wolf lunch down in an attempt to catch the last ten minutes, or should one stage a scene and refuse to eat until it was over? I imagine that in 1973 I attempted my usual untidy compromise, darting out between bites to catch a snatch of Sweet singing 'Blockbuster', before being bawled back in again.

Last night, for the first time in 18 years, I was able to see what I had missed. 'The Sweet have had a fan-tastic year,' said Tony Blackburn. The Sweet then performed 'Blockbuster' wearing a selection of gold jumpsuits, sparkle, red satin loon pants and foot-high platform heels. 'Fan-tastic,' said Tony. Dawn then sang 'Tie a Yellow Ribbon'. Tony said: 'Gilbert O'Sullivan's had a fan-tastic year.' Pan's People danced to 'Get Down', dressed in platform heels and what looked like maternity smocks, with much animated arm circling and facial expression on the phrase 'Happy as can be!' Next, Gary Glitter sang 'Leader of the Gang', looking rather like an oven-ready Terry Scott in aluminium foil. While Tony was saying, 'What a fan-tastic year it's been for Peters and Lee,' I began to realise that despite it all I was enjoying every second, and I thanked God that my youth hadn't coincided with a period of good taste.

As Wizzard sang 'I Wish It Could Be Christmas Every Day', my wife came in and said, 'Does it have to be this loud?', the very same question my father used to ask all those years ago. My happiness was complete. 'That was Wizzard,' said Tony. 'Weren't they fan-tastic?'

A couple of hours later, *Christmas Night with the Stars* from 1964 seemed impossibly ancient. There were times when I expected it to be followed by a Christmas Message from King Alfred the Great. Billy Cotton kicked it all off with a shout of 'Wakey! Wakey!' and a rendition of 'Food, Glorious Food', waddling around with a carving knife and fork while girls in shortie gingham aprons danced around a kitchen table. 'Well, no need to tell you that that was Billy Cotton,' said Jack Warner, compèring. 'Billy's one of our oldest friends – no offence, Bill!'

Kathy Kirby sang 'Silent Night', the Black and White Minstrels a high-spirited medley including 'South of the Border', and Ralph Reader's Boy Scout Gangshow a song in praise of walking, which went: 'A motor car is phoney/I'd rather have Shanks's pony'. Ah, such innocence, such naivety, such utter ghastliness! And why did so many Boy Scouts in those days look like the Kray brothers?

parents will have completed installation of the equivalent of nineteen forklift truckloads of parcels, and the children can now gleefully set about trashing this second tranche. Included in this will be many of the smaller items: cars with screeching alarms, babies that cry their hearts out and, for all I know, toy puppies that will perform a convincingly natural poop (complete with pong) all over your fitted carpet. Nevertheless, if a few of these are left lying around when the next wave of guests arrives, you may find the house clearing faster than if you'd fed cabbage-water to a cocker spaniel.

From this point, it will be impossible to cross from any one part of your home to any other part, as the path of paper, ribbons and expanded polystyrene is just too treacherous for someone with a schooner of sherry on board. Faced with this challenge, Sir Ranulph Twisleton-Wykeham Fiennes would turn tail and race back to the Antarctic. You need also to be aware that from this point onwards, you will see neither the television remote control nor the double-issue *Radio Times* which you spent all last night studying and marking up. Furthermore, the only people who know how to change channels will be the under-tens, because nowadays one of the first things they learn with their nursery vouchers is how to rip off the front panel of a Sony Trinitron and operate from first principles.

They have also absorbed the details of linking up their computer – even in a stranger's home – so now, along with missing the Queen's Speech and *It'll Be Alright on the Night*, you will be sentenced to nine hours of non-stop peeping, bleeping, buzzing and inanely jingling video games. Believe me, after all that, you'll appreciate that there is actually nothing remotely 'super' about the Mario Brothers. A short while from now, you may consider retiring into a glass of soluble aspirin (see the section on Drugs).

The next grasping freeloader to expect a come-hither will be the vicar or priest, who firmly believes that he is as hysterical as *Father Ted* and twice as cute as the cast of *Ballykissangel*. To him you can graciously say that he is most welcome to join all the family fun after Christmas lunch … no, it's absolutely no inconvenience as we were looking for one extra male to join in Naked Twister, after which we thought we might have a seance when we'll be trying to reach family members 'on

Showing the tell-tale signs that you're sick of Christmas?

☆ You start baking hot cross buns on Boxing Day.

☆ You've got red-and-green bags under your eyes.

☆ You start laughing hysterically halfway through *The Snowman*.

☆ You're looking up recipes for reindeer fricassee.

☆ During a family game of Cluedo, you start to plan the perfect murder.

☆ You no longer 'get' Morecambe and Wise.

☆ You wish for once Julie Andrews would just slap those kids.

☆ Even your fingernails taste a little like turkey.

☆ Granny's Brussels-sprout farts just aren't funny any more.

☆ You take down the tinsel and replace it with barbed wire.

☆ You start to find your relatives really interesting people.

☆ You wish Wallace and Gromit would land in a blender.

☆ You cheer during *The Great Escape* when Donald Sutherland gets recaptured after saying 'goodbye' in English.

You're Not Alone
CALL FOR HELP 0100 00 00 00

the other side' to offer them the compliments of the season.

Once all the arrangements have been sorted out, you'll need a very carefully thought-out table-plan. This can take considerable time and effort if it is to have the desired effect of leading swiftly to walk-outs, frayed tempers and bad language. Start by making sure that you alternate the very young and the very old, which ensures that nobody has anything in common with the person next to them, and that the young guests have to repeat everything at least three

times before the old guests understand what they're saying, by which time their patience has snapped. A variant on this idea is to check everyone's star sign, then with the help of an astrological chart, make sure each person is sitting next to someone quite incompatible – if you're not sure, it's

usually their own star sign that people find most objectionable! For individual flare-ups, it's helpful to revisit old wounds, so couples who have recently divorced, or are about to, are a safe bet. Also, brothers and sisters usually fight like terriers. And remember to assess the situation constantly throughout the meal. If things are going too well, make an instant rearrangement – it's a reasonable assumption that a college student who's recently taken to body-piercing, experimenting with soft drugs and exploring his own multifaceted sexuality is not going to hit it off with an over-fifty Justice of the Peace who's just taken her advanced motorist test and is standing for president of the local WRVS.

On occasion, you may need to break the ice, and I've often found that an off-colour joke can help things along. Avoid mother-in-law stories, as there are bound to be at least two sitting at the table. And anything to do with Alzheimer's may upset Grandpa … if he understands!! Why not come out with: 'I played a terrible round of golf yesterday. The only two good balls I hit were when I stood on a rake.' The reaction to this will give you the measure of the party, and you can take it from there or retreat into elephant-and-fridge jokes. Another method to help people overcome their initial embarrassment is to wait until someone leaves the table to go to the loo. Upon their return, ask cheerily: 'Could you hear us while you were in there?' Save them from their sheepish awkwardness by chortling heartily: 'Because we could hear you!'

As the meal draws to a close, it's always a nice gesture to have a surprise announcement ready for the delight of everyone present. The host or hostess will

WAYS TO RUIN A CHILD'S CHRISTMAS

NEW MEMBERS ENTITLED TO ONE OFFER FROM THIS INCREDIBLE LIST!
HURRY! – OFFER LIMITED TO ONE OPTION PER HOUSEHOLD

- Point out casually that Santa is in fact an anagram of Satan.
- Take them to Santa's grottiest grotto and carefully explain that it's just some over-the-hill actor with a fake beard who'd rather be an extra in the Rover's Return.
- Buy them a bicycle, but tell them they've got to share it.
- Tell them solemnly on Christmas morning that you *did* buy them a puppy but it got sick and died. Maybe you wrapped it up too tightly …
- Serve lunch five minutes before the end of Christmas Day *EastEnders*.
- Send them away on a 'Discover the Spirit of Christmas Past' theme week. Bed and board in an authentic workhouse.
- Presents are out this year. You've donated a sum to charity on their behalf. Point out that you've given them the best gift a child could ever receive at Christmas – a conscience.
- Stage a Christmas Eve burglary. All they'll find is some discarded bits of wrapping paper. (And you can claim on the insurance.)
- Tell them in no uncertain terms that Buzz Lightyear was all the rage last year and it's time to get real.
- Tuck them up in bed on Christmas Eve and then tell them that Grandpa and Grandma are getting a divorce.
- Leave them home alone and fly off to Barbados with your local singles club.
- Tell them to make the most of the day's festivities because tomorrow we're all moving to Albania. And yes, you will have to change schools.
- Threaten them with a trip to Eurodisney in six feet of snow.
- Offer more Brussels sprouts.
- Introduce the notion of irony: Santa does not exist, but Noel Edmonds does!
- Thrash him/her at Nintendo.
- Explain that Granny's voucher for a year's piano lessons will be a very useful present.
- Refuse to change channels from UK Gold.
- Keep saying 'You'll grow into it'.

JOIN THE SCROOGE SOCIETY TODAY!
If YOU'VE got what it takes to help, please send a donation

A little bit of misery goes a long way

always keep something back for the end of a party, preferably accompanied by a special culinary treat like *petits fours* or a vintage Armagnac. You will need to find out something special about one of your guests, and make a solemn point by tapping your glass for silence, then announcing: 'Not many people know this, but I have it on good authority that Doreen has just had a very successful hysterectomy. So raise your glasses in a toast.' It could be a younger member of the household who is perhaps rather too shy to share his happiness with everyone publicly, so you can help out by saying something along these lines: 'Now, we've all known Christopher since he was a few hours old, and that doesn't seem so long ago! Ha ha. But now that he's nineteen, I'm sure he'd appreciate it if you would all join me now in congratulating him on his coming out.' Don't be surprised if his mother faints and his father leaves slamming the door, for this is merely the heightened emotion of a very thrilling moment for them. I do know this, because people have often tapped me on the back after an event such as this and congratulated me on having 'dropped a real bombshell' … which is surely what throwing good parties is all about.

LUCKY SANTA

A GROUP of children saw a helicopter bringing Santa Claus to their Palm Beach party crash in flames. Luckily Santa was rescued by the pilot.

Daily Express 17/12/96

With all this excitement going on, it's quite likely that at some point during lunch Roger will nip upstairs. The purpose of this will have nothing to do with nature's plumbing requisites, but will enable him to pick up the bedroom extension in order to telephone his mistress, who's staying two hundred miles away with her mother. The best way to cause humiliation (and possibly a decree nisi!) is to make sure the baby monitor is turned on to full volume before tapping your glass with a knife once more to command hushed reverence while he bills and coos at her unawares!

As soon as the meal is over, you promise yourself 'five minutes sit-down' before you do the washing up (since no one has offered, except Gran, whose idea of washing-up is not dissimilar to Swampy's idea of a good bath). So, you tramp into the lounge, recover the remote control (try the waste bin first) and settle back (not in your favourite armchair, as this will be occupied by carrycot and a Labrador) to enjoy a little television. But don't tune in expecting to discover the residents of Albert Square exchanging merry festive Cockney banter. Far from it! In the battle for ratings, Christmas soaps have become the province of high drama. At the very least, you should expect a murder in the snug of the Rover's Return, or a brutal sexual attack at the Korner Kabin. I think it's appalling, although if they ever scripted a nuclear accident on Brookside Close, that might be worth a look.

Even if you *are* able to veto the soaps, you may find it more difficult to escape *Top of the Pops*, which will be on one or other of the BBC channels for most of the two days. For those of you unfamiliar with the pop charts, I shall offer this concise guide:

1 Christmas is a time when all traditional values of artistry and musicality can be thrown aside, with the prize going to the most irritating and banal song released in the previous month. You might like to think of it as a kind of Festivision Song Contest. Hot favourite will be a novelty record, which will be a 'Christmas Song' ... although unarguably 'Christmas', this is only arguably a 'song'.

2 The late-December chart will also contain a number of re-entries – the twenty or so hardy perennials, also known as pension plans for seventies bands like Slade and Mud. Many of these bands are boxed up in Micky Most's garage for eleven months of the year until ready to be released on their Xmas tour.

3 Next comes a record by the latest Big Thing. Here, the act in question will not waste a good single because the Christmas chart is such a lottery. Instead, they will plug an obscure, generally slow track from their last album, adding tinsel to the cover and sleigh bells to the middle eight.

4 Cliff Richard will be in the programme at some point. So will Elton John. So will a group of has-beens who have made a charidee record.

GRANDMA GOT RUN OVER BY A REINDEER

by Randy Brooks

CHORUS
*Grandma got run over by a reindeer
Walking home from our house Christmas Eve.
You can say there's no such thing as Santa,
But as for me an' Grandpa, we believe.*

She'd been drinking too much eggnog,
And we begged her not to go.
But she forgot her medication,
And she staggered out the door into the snow.

When we found her Christmas morning,
At the scene of the attack
She had hoof prints on her forehead,
And incriminating Claus marks on her back.

CHORUS
*Now we're all so proud of Grandpa,
He's been taking this so well.
See him in there watching football,
Drinking beer and playing cards with cousin Mel.*

It's not Christmas without Grandma,
All the family's dressed in black.
And we just can't help but wonder
Should we open up her gifts or send them back?
SEND THEM BACK!!!

CHORUS
*Now the goose is on the table
And the pudding made of fig (aahhh!)
And the blue and silver candles,
That would just have matched the hair in Grandma's wig.*

I've warned all my friends and neighbours,
Better watch out for yourselves.
They should never give a licence,
To a man who drives a sleigh and plays with elves.

Sing it, Grandpa!

CHORUS

5 To avoid Christmas chart music altogether, do not enter any high-street shop or supermarket. At all costs, do not tune in to any radio station after mid-October. Good luck.

A traditional alternative to television and radio, though not often enough used these days, is to wheel out the slide projector and the old Super 8 machine, and offer to remind all the gathered clan of the joys of Christmas past. About four minutes into the first film, comment loudly how much younger everyone looked then. If that hasn't shifted them, head straight for the photograph album, and the page containing the naked paddling-pool shots. Suddenly, there'll be an urgent need around the room to find coats, hats, gloves, car keys …

Someone will have suggested a walk, and this is often met with not entirely spontaneous or convincing enthusiasm. But why not combine the walk with a little extra activity, and arrange some carol singing? Little preparation is needed, as the words to one carol will be quite adequate, if learned by all participants. There are, however, some golden rules which you should stick to:

- Know the first four lines of your carol and practise these. The rest don't matter, as the door will either open by the time you finish the first verse, or you'll hear something like 'bugger off' clearly through the letterbox.
- If you feel you are not welcome, repeat the first four lines ad nauseam until you have made your point and the householders begin to scream hysterically.
- Ring the doorbell once. Then again. And again.
- Make sure you have a large bucket, otherwise they will think you expect only a small coin. Always have change for a large note, though never more than half its value.

Keep an eye on the clock. Make sure you finish at least half an hour before the pubs close. This will give you time to count your takings, and bag the coppers nicely for the landlord, who will welcome the change and greet you with open arms and a selection of his finest ales.

Once the kitty is spent, if there is not enough left over to buy one last drink, place the remaining coins in the charity box on the bar.

R. WILSON ESQ. SCROOGE VILLAS HUMBUG STREET LONDON SW1 2PN

6th January

Dear Radio Times

It was great to see all the TV channels keeping the Christmas traditions alive this year, I especially enjoyed the Christmas TV repeats of:

One Foot in the Grave (any Christmas special of this programme is worth seeing again!)
It'll Be Alright on the Night,   Auntie's Bloomers,
Morecambe and Wise, The Likely Lads,
Steptoe and Son, Hancock's Half Hour,
The Sound of Music, The Great Escape,
The Wizard of Oz, Gone with the Wind,
  Dr Zhivago, Lawrence of Arabia
Brief Encounter, Only Fools and Horses,
  The Queen's Speech, The Snowman,
Carols from King's College, You've Been Framed,
and last but by no means least Wallace and Gromit

In my opinion, any repeat is a good idea, anything to keep the cost of the licence down.

Yours faithfully

R. Wilson

Or, who knows, you may be spared having guests at all this year. But this can mean only one thing. You have decided to visit THE IN-LAWS. In all likelihood, you'll have been arguing since Midsummer's Eve about which set of the in-laws to visit, since it's a law of nature – jester that she is – that every couple has TWO sets of the bloody things. Usually, the choice is determined by which set had the visit last year, though this is often complicated by the argument that one of the two mothers-in-law is the better cook … or has the bigger house … or lives forty miles nearer … or doesn't have a golden retriever that's just had a litter of eleven.

In-laws are like spent nuclear fuel rods: nobody quite knows what to do with them, and even fewer people know what exact purpose they once served, but everyone knows they contaminate any environment, and have a half-life that stays with you longer than the odour of a teenager's trainers. Trying to forget you're going to see the in-laws is like trying to forget that you're going to die.

Having accepted the fact that – in the suffering stakes – it makes little difference on which set of in-laws you bestow your company, fate (or, more likely, your beloved spouse) enters the arena to make the final decision for you. And, as your car draws gingerly up Mother-in-law's drive at midday, you know you would feel happier about driving your family to Freddie Krueger's house. The front-door is ajar, the holly wreath dangling precariously from the knocker, a trail of red sauce with trampled-in berries leads the way into the kitchen where a still-solid turkey is sweating unstuffed on the

kitchen table. The next-door neighbour is trying to mend the tree lights as the smoke alarm signals that the potatoes are almost done. Father-in-law thinks nobody knows he's watching a 'busty' video he won last night in the pub, accompanied by his fifth pre-lunch mug of cider (he still imagines the kids think it's apple juice). Meanwhile, their grandchildren are giving a passable impersonation of the ragamuffin cast of *Oliver!* breaking toys left, right and centre, tearing at each other's hair, opening bags of crisps and shouting 'more, more, more'. Accept it and prepare. It will be messy. You will need J-cloths. Christmas at the in-laws is a scene that makes Dante's Inferno look like Blackpool pleasure beach.

And, when you do finally pull up at their house on Christmas Day or Boxing Day, they will have just had a blazing row. Don't worry, this is a seasonal tradition which has been practised in Britain for centuries. Whatever you do, it's not worth attempting to lighten the atmosphere right away. Instead, try to locate your bedrooms and start unpacking. Mind you, this is not as straightforward as it sounds, since several of you will be sharing the living room, and the kids will have to pretend that the kitchen table is a bunk bed. Nothing, however, will dislodge your in-laws from their master *en suite* bedroom, unless you are able to produce a medical certificate which says you will be left permanently disabled if you have to sleep on a sofa bed.

If, after half an hour, matters show no sign of improving – for example, neither party has offered to put on the kettle – then suddenly remember that you heard an emergency shipping forecast in the car as you were driving down, and what with the hurricanes, snowstorms and avalanches heading this way, you think it better if you put the family back in the car and make for home while the roads are still open. For those who don't like to tell such fibs, why not arrange to have the visit curtailed by the in-laws themselves. Some preparation is required, whereby you must feed your pet pooch with extremely rich creamy food and mashed sprouts for a few days before setting off. On arrival, bring the dog in from the car, and place him on the hearth-rug with the words: 'He hasn't stopped being sick all the way from home.

But I'm sure he's as right as rain now.' If it's a cat you've brought with you, their reaction will be all the more instant.

Once Father-in-law's been down to the shed for the two loungers and the dodgy deckchair, and you've all found a seat, liven things up by saying that you've been given a marvellous book as a present by someone at work, then offer to read from it. Their faces will look as though they've sucked a lemon when you go on to inform them that the title is *The Collected Works of Patience Strong*. However, just in case you have the kind of in-laws who are appreciative of these lovely poems (probably the religious type) you could try telling them it's *The Bumper Book of Rugby Songs* instead.

By now, you may all be in need of some outside diversion, so take a quick look in the local paper to see if there's a circus nearby, since in my experience the average Christmas circus show lasts only marginally less time than a performance of the complete works of Shakespeare, and has the same soporific effect. Do wrap up well, though, as the temperature inside the tent will be low enough to freeze the nuts off the Forth Bridge. If the circus isn't in town, I'm sure there'll be a panto within fifty miles. Being of a theatrical persuasion, I like to visit the occasional panto to see what my dear colleagues are forced to do to avoid financial ruin during the intervening ten and a half months of the year when they claim they are so tired that they are 'resting'. Poor loves. A panto is the ideal theatrical event for traumatising young children for a very long time. I advise a seat on the aisle for one of the youngsters, then come the moment when the dame decides 'she' needs a helping hand with one of her ridiculous songs, simply shove the little terror up on to the stage with all your force. The sheer horror that grips them at the point of contact with this hideous advertisement for transvestism will stay with them for many, many years. A word of warning, however: in extreme cases there can be long spells of rather expensive psychotherapy lasting well into adulthood as a result of this encounter.

Simpler and more cost-effective expeditions could be arranged to a local DIY superstore, though care must be taken here to ensure that there is absolutely nothing on display that the children could want you to buy for them. You are clearly living in a fantasy world if you imagine that they will have had enough of lavish presents merely because it's twenty-four hours after Christmas Day.

POLITICALLY CORRECT SANTA

by Harvey Ehrlich

'Twas the night before Christmas, and Santa's a wreck …
How to live in a world that's politically correct?
His workers no longer would answer to 'Elves',
'Vertically Challenged' they were calling themselves.

And labour conditions at the north pole
Were challenged by the union to stifle the soul.
Four reindeer had vanished, without much propriety,
Released to the wilds by the Humane Society.
And equal employment had made it quite clear
That Santa had better not use just reindeer.
So Dancer and Donner, Comet and Cupid,
Were replaced with four pigs, and you know that looked stupid!

The runners had been removed from his sleigh;
The ruts were termed dangerous by the EPA.
And people had started to call for the cops
When they heard sled noises on their rooftops.
Second-hand smoke from his pipe had his workers quite frightened.

His fur-trimmed red suit was called 'unenlightened'.
And to show you the strangeness of life's ebbs and flows,
Rudolf was suing over unauthorised use of his nose
And had gone on Geraldo, in front of the nation,
Demanding millions in overdue compensation.

So, half of the reindeer were gone; and his wife,
Who suddenly said she'd enough of this life,
Joined a self-help group, packed, and left in a whiz,
Demanding from now on her title was Ms.
And, as for the gifts, why, he'd ne'er had a notion
That making a choice could cause so much commotion.
Nothing of leather, nothing of fur,
Which meant nothing for him. And nothing for her.

Nothing that might be construed to pollute.
Nothing to aim. Nothing to shoot.
Nothing that clamoured or made lots of noise.
Nothing for just girls. Or just for the boys.

Nothing that claimed to be gender specific.
Nothing that's warlike or non-pacific.
No candy or sweets … they were bad for the tooth.
Nothing that seemed to embellish a truth.

And fairy tales, while not yet forbidden,
Were like Ken and Barbie, better off hidden.

For they raised the hackles of those psychological
Who claimed the only good gift was one ecological.

No baseball, no football … someone could get hurt;
Besides, playing sports exposed kids to dirt.
Dolls were said to be sexist, and should be passé;
And Nintendo would rot your entire brain away.

So Santa just stood there, dishevelled, perplexed;
He just could not figure out what to do next.
He tried to be merry, tried to be gay,
But you've got to be careful with that word today.

His sack was quite empty, limp to the ground;
Nothing fully acceptable was to be found.
Something special was needed, a gift that he might
Give to all without angering the left or the right.

A gift that would satisfy, with no indecision,
Each group of people, every religion;
Every ethnicity, every hue,
Everyone, everywhere … even you.

So here is that gift, it's price beyond worth …
'May you and your loved ones enjoy peace on earth.'

RELIGION

For some unaccountable reason, religion has, over the years, been allowed to creep gradually in to what until recently was kept as a deeply commercial time. Despite the best efforts of the retail trade and of television schedulers, there are still those for whom Christmas is principally a sanctified event. If you are the kind of person who attends church for christenings, weddings and funerals but then, for the rest of the year, uses it just as a convenient place to park the car, you may benefit from the following advice before heading off on Christmas Eve for your annual visit to the popular, beautiful (and, dare I say, rather theatrical) ceremony called Midnight Mass.

Firstly, know with whom you are dealing. Vicars are normally easy to spot, even if they are part of the 'plain-clothes clergy' who have eschewed the dog-collar in favour of an open-necked shirt and jazzy cardigan … who see themselves as a communicator first, vicar second … and who are determined to capture a larger audience, even if that means going 'happy clappy' or downmarket. With or without their cycle clips, if you ever come across this kind of ecclesiastical Noel Edmonds, you will have no difficulty in recognising them.

Enough of the shepherd, what about his flock? Well, the only parishioners likely to cause you any *real* trouble are the recent converts, those who popped into Tesco for some kitchen towel, and quite unexpectedly found themselves overcome by the Spirit of the Lord somewhere south of the oven chips. I generally find that born-again Christians have much in common with lifelong smokers who, having finally quit, now wear T-shirts emblazoned with the No Smoking symbol. The type that expects everyone to extinguish their cigarettes as they pass in the street – rather as I myself do, in fact! Look out for these new recruits within a group of carol singers, or handing round the collection plates with a big smile at the end of each pew. They will feel it is vital to grin at each passing shopper, which will make it quite impossible for them to follow the words on their carol sheet. So apart from bawling the odd phrase they remember from school assembly, they will otherwise mime like a *Top of the Pops* debutant.

I must confess, though, I do quite like carols. After all, the tunes are very catchy. But whatever the temptation, you must never join in, as this will immediately attract the attention of those shaking the collection boxes. If you are inadvertently caught out, in most cases it should be possible to outrun them, assuming you're not laden down with parcels ... and you won't be if you have followed my guidance so far. I would, however, warn you against taking on any member of the Salvation Army, as this uniformed branch of the Church is a formidable strike force. This God Squad even *sings* with a certain authority. I mean, look at Thora Hird in maroon serge – would you cross her? The most highly trained officers – the SAS of the SA, if you like – will have been sent out from the body of the group, and will move among the shoppers like Stealth bombers. Any attempt to escape will be met with a rapid response: generally, a pincer movement driving you back towards the ranks of the band, where you risk becoming impaled on a slide trombone. Take this advice: just keep some spare foreign coins in your pocket for these eventualities, pay up as noisily as possible to make it sound as though you have dropped in a big lottery win, then move along quietly.

By now you may have guessed that I do have a sneaking respect for the Church community – call it old-fashioned, call it sentimental, call it my Calvinist upbringing, whatever. When all's said and done, it cannot be easy encouraging each new generation to become involved with the Church, particularly now that they've started showing *Grange Hill* on Sunday mornings. And besides, if you really are feeling the strain over Christmas, maybe Church is precisely the kind of sanctuary you need from the hurly-burly. If this is so, then you will have no shortage of opportunities:

Christmas Eve

4 p.m.

The Children's Service, which by rights will include the blessing of the Nativity Scene. This is always rather spectacular (and a bit tearful, if the truth be known) as babies and young children get to grips with the fantastic acoustic potential of a church. You will *never* have heard crying like this.

6 p.m.

With barely time for the churchwardens to clean up the sick and dispose of the Pampers, the church is reopened for the traditional service of nine lessons, two mince-pies, one sherry and carols. Here, though, you ought to be aware that many parishes set traps for the unsuspecting newcomer. For example, you should prepare to miss out the last verse of 'O Come All Ye Faithful' and (unless you're a lady) also the first verse of the chorus. And, whatever you do, do *not* join in on the first verse of 'Once in Royal David's City' as the head chorister has been promised this prize all year long, and indeed may have fought hard for the privilege ... in a choirboy kind of way, you understand. Simply enjoy as he crackles and warbles his way through his party piece, and comes to terms with one of the more disagreeable and unpredictable aspects of puberty.

NB: If done properly, this service could take a fair old time, so help yourself to some of the cushions scattered around the floor, and place one beneath your posterior and another behind your spinal column, otherwise you may be spending Christmas with the osteopath.

11.30 p.m.

Midnight Mass, when (apologising for the incongruous imagery) *all hell is let loose*. However, this is an interesting allegory, for the fight of good and evil will be waged in the flesh as the churchwardens attempt to dissuade the town drunks from rejoining the queue for communion wine, explaining that the small 'nibbles' represent the body of Christ, and that 'whatever Sir's preference, on this occasion pork scratchings just would not be appropriate'. Even the most worship-ful parishioners will have had a rather merry evening already, and will not be able to remember whether they arrived at church by Sierra or sandal. The collection plate will never have been so full … neither will the pews. Beware worshipping false idols – at some point around 12.30 a.m., you will begin to feel a strange glow, as though Christmas was rather special after all. Pull yourself together … it will all seem as ghastly as ever by tomorrow morning.

Christmas Morning

8 a.m.

The church is opened for an early communion, and to allow those who fell asleep during Midnight Mass to find their way back home. This being Christmas Day, the infant Jesus is added to the Nativity scene, while the half-emptied bottles of lager are removed.

I doubt it will be all that long before things return to normal, and we're not besieged with religiosity during what should be a nice peaceful winter holiday. You may already have heard that there are some very high-rolling bids to purchase all the rights to Christmas, from the likes of Tesco, Disney and even the Microsoft Corporation. What exactly they will be buying is anybody's guess, though I tend to believe the rumours that suggest the date will be moved to July or August, which makes a lot of sense, considering that the weather's better and the kids will be on school holidays. And the traditional story would still work, of course. I mean, why would it be any easier for Mary and Joseph to find a hotel room in the middle of the high season? The only aspect that bothers me slightly about all this is the need for a revamped Messiah figure, somebody who will be a more modern icon for the kiddies. I perhaps ought to confess that I myself was under consideration for the part, until it was felt that a bearded celebrity would present a more appropriate image, combining the look of Jesus with the 'lovability factor' of Santa Claus. There is a secret list of candidates doing the rounds, and I have no hesitation in sharing it with you, so that you are aware what is in store and are able to take the necessary precautions.

Bob Geldof	Mike Gatting	Zak Dingle
Jeremy Beadle	Brian Blessed	Matthew Kelly
Richard Branson	Richard Stilgoe	Robin Cook
k d lang	Barry White	David Bellamy

Sometimes, you just hope things will stay as they are!

CHRISTMAS AT WORK

Arguably the only drawback about the traditional office party is the traditional necessity to start writing job applications the morning after. When all's said and done, it's the only party where someone else pays for all the booze, where none of the guests has to do the washing up and probably the only occasion each year when you'll have the opportunity to talk animatedly and amusingly to people with whom you have never exchanged a word over the previous twelve months.

It may also be the occasion when, if you keep your mind off the rum punch and the secretaries' legs, you may be able to win that promotion you've always longed for. Take along a Polaroid camera, a bottle of Polish spirit and a clump of mistletoe to the merry-making. Hand out liberal quantities of the 78% proof and mistletoe, and snap any outcome that involves senior management … or, even better, the MD himself. With blackmailing material safely in hand, a smooth transition up the career ladder is assured.

Otherwise, work at this time of year can be hell. People will start dressing up in silly costumes and shake buckets of coins at you in the name of charity. Whenever I see them coming, I'm tempted to ejaculate like my old Uncle Scrooge: 'Are there no workhouses?' People from different departments will start sending you cards with signatures you can't make out. Suppliers will shower you with the most useless items ever invented by marketing departments, such as wall planners on which no pen yet invented can write, or pencil pots with illegibly small calendars for this year, next year and the year after that printed around the base. Customers will expect to be lavished with bottles of port and rounds of Stilton, or they'll cheerily ring you for the first time in weeks – not to place an order or to settle an outstanding invoice, but to hint that they might be free to attend a Christmas lunch at the most expensive restaurant in the region.

But beneath all this reprehensible behaviour comes the most subhuman of all, whereby bosses are fuelled by the words 'Season of Goodwill', and decide to make closer contact with their secretaries – professionally speaking, needless to say.

They'll start offering them perfume ... lunch ... flowers ... days off ... dinner ... the company chauffeur for a couple of hours' shopping in town. Bosses will also, for the first time all year, display an unwholesome interest in the operation of the photocopier, usually around the time of the annual office party. For some reason they will wish to do something 'in private', then be seen fumbling for the enlargement function ... presumably so as to reduce their embarrassment.

Other ranks may wait until the office party itself is in full swing before revealing their true colours. Dancing at the party will be more Strictly Boardroom than Ballroom, so choose your partners carefully and avoid the General Manager, who will be performing a perfect Macarena in the middle of the floor ... while the 'Birdy Song' is playing. The Finance Director usually has the dance-floor presence of a man who thinks the Lambada is a company car, while the twenty-three-year-old post room assistant seems to be trying to improve his line dancing. At least, that's what someone said when they saw him coming out of the gents' for the fifth time blowing his nose. The ultimate embarrassment is often reserved for the newest personal assistant, who will be expected to have the last dance with one of the more lascivious company directors. It will certainly not be the kind of rise she had been hoping for this year.

HINTS FOR SURVIVING THE OFFICE PARTY

1 Male workers should avoid going to the toilet at the same time as their boss. As you stand side by side at the urinal, you will discover that not only has he no understanding of the concept of 'defensible space', neither does he have any idea who you are.

2 If you insist on photocopying your backside, take a precaution. Before doing so, add a few unmistakable distinguishing marks. That way, you'll be in the clear should the incident be referred to an industrial tribunal. 'Your Honour, my client's reputation is spotless, as indeed is his bottom. I would go so far as to say it is as spotless as Lord Archer's spinal regions.'

Desperate Pick-up Lines to Use at the Office Party

Would you like to unwrap something of mine?

I promise you these baubles aren't made of glass

Fancy joining me in the sack?

I've got something you can hang a wreath on

Why of course I've come to fill your stocking

See what I mean ... it's not all padding.

YES, THAT IS AN ELF IN MY PANTS.. WANNA SEE HIM?

The turkey's not the only one who could do with a good stuffing.

Of course, you're the only Christmas Cracker I want to pull.

Yes, it's me who puts the screw in Scrooge.

3 Plan escape routes that bypass all mistletoe, but keep a sprig in your pocket in case you should wish to surprise anybody in the lift.

4 If, despite the free booze, you decide you want to avoid it altogether, first make all the party arrangements. (Better still, chair the committee that makes the party arrangements.) Then, when you shamelessly skive off that day, no one will be remotely suspicious of your deceit. Simply call the boss's secretary first thing, and suggest you will try to make it to the office later on. But leave strict instructions that they must 'soldier on' without you.

Amazingly, in this profligate period, a Christmas lunch is often regarded as a business necessity on top of the office party! Restaurants during the month of December are packed to the lavatory doors with screeching works outings, and nothing exasperates the staff more than yet another party of whingeing office workers celebrating Yuletide. With this in mind, make sure you:

- Ask for *no Brussels sprouts* with your meal (they'll have to pick them out)
- Claim you ordered *still* mineral water for forty, not fizzy (which will already be open)
- Request a dessert not on the menu, such as summer fruits cheesecake
- Get riotously drunk
- Wear a ridiculous party hat
- Ask if they could divide the bill by forty-one, but point out that one person didn't have a main course and two didn't have a starter
- Dance on the table before being sick under it
- Leave absolutely no tip

If the waiters and waitresses do not smile and wish you good night as you leave, report them to the manager. Christmas cheer all round!!

A Christmas Poem

by Wendy Cope

At Christmas
little children sing
and merry bells jingle,

The cold winter air makes
our hands and faces tingle,

And happy families go to church
and cheerily they mingle,

And the whole business is unbelievably
dreadful, if you're single.

CHRISTMAS OFFICE MEMO

by Phillip Winn

Memorandum

To: All employees of Christmas, Inc.
Re: Downsizing

Season's Greetings. The recent announcement that Donner and Blitzen have elected to take the early reindeer retirement package has triggered a good deal of concern about whether they will be replaced, and about other restructuring decisions here at the North Pole.

Streamlining was appropriate in view of the reality that the North Pole no longer dominates the season's gift distribution business. Home shopping channels and mail order catalogues have diminished Santa's market share and he could not sit idly by and permit further erosion of the profit picture.

The reindeer downsizing was made possible through the purchase of a late model Japanese sled for the CEO's annual trip. Improved productivity through Dasher and Dancer, who summered at the Harvard Business School, is anticipated and should take up the slack with no discernible loss of service. Reduction in reindeer will also lessen airborne environmental emissions for which the North Pole has been cited and received unfavourable press.

I am pleased to inform you that Rudolph's role will not be disturbed. Tradition still counts for something at the North Pole. Management denies, in the strongest possible language, the earlier leak that Rudolph's nose got that way not because of the cold, but from substance abuse. Calling Rudolph "a lush who was into the sauce and never did pull his share of the load" was an unfortunate comment, made by one of Santa's helpers and taken out of context at a time of year when he is known to be under executive stress. As a further restructuring, today's global challenges require the North Pole to continue to look for better, more competitive steps to take. Effective immediately, the following economy measures are to take place in the "Twelve Days Of Christmas" subsidiary:

The partridge will be retained, but the pear tree never turned out to be the cash crop forecast. It will be replaced by a plastic hanging plant, providing considerable savings in maintenance.

The two turtle doves represent a redundancy that is simply not cost effective. In addition, their romance during working hours could not be condoned. Their positions are eliminated.

The three French hens will be eliminated. After all, nobody likes the French.

cont.

The four calling birds have been replaced by an automated voice mail system, with a call-waiting option. An analysis is underway to determine who the birds have been calling, how often, and how long they talked.

The five golden rings have been put on hold by the Board of Directors. Maintaining a portfolio on one commodity could have negative implications for our institutional investors. Diversification into other precious metals as well as a mix of T-Bills and high technology stock appears to be in order.

The six geese-a-laying constitute a luxury which can no longer be afforded. It has been long felt that the production rate of one egg per goose per day is an example of the decline in productivity. Three geese will be let go, and an upgrading in the selection procedure by Personnel will assure management that from now on every goose it gets will be a good one.

The seven swans-a-swimming is obviously a number chosen in better times. The function is primarily decorative. Mechanical swans are on order. The current swans will be retrained to learn some new strokes, enhancing their outplacement potential.

As you know, the eight maids-a-milking concept has been under heavy scrutiny by the EEOC. A male/female balance in the workforce is being sought. The more militant maids consider this a dead-end job with no upward mobility. Automation of the process may permit the maids to try a-mending, a-mentoring, or a-mulching.

Nine ladies dancing has always been an odd number. This function will be phased out as these individuals grow older and can no longer do the steps.

Ten lords-a-leaping is overkill. The high cost of the lords, plus the expense of international air travel, prompted the Compensation Committee to suggest replacing this group with ten out-of-work lawyers. While leaping ability may be somewhat sacrificed, the savings are significant because we expect an oversupply of unemployed lawyers this year and the next.

Eleven pipers piping and twelve drummers drumming is a simple case of the band getting too big. Substituting a string quartet, cutting back on new music, and no uniforms will produce savings which drop right to the bottom line.

Thus we can expect a substantial reduction in assorted people, fowl, animals, and other expenses. Also, though incomplete, studies indicate that stretching deliveries over twelve days is inefficient. If we can drop-ship in one day, service levels will be improved. Regarding the attorney's association lawsuit seeking expansion to include the legal profession ("thirteen lawyers-a-suing"), action is still pending. If put into effect, the Compensation Committee's proposal should help.

Lastly, it is not beyond consideration that deeper cuts may be necessary in the future to stay competitive. If that happens, the Board will request management to strictly scrutinise the "Snow White" division to see if seven dwarves is still the right number.

THINGS TO DO TODAY

— COMPLETE MY INLAND REVENUE SELF-ASSESSMENT FORMS.

— LAY A PATIO.

— MAKE PUFF PASTRY.

— SUGAR-SOAP THE BEDROOM WALLS.

— OIL THE LAWNMOWER BLADES.

— WASH OUT THE DUSTBINS.

— REMOVE THE HAIR FROM ALL THE U-BENDS IN THE HOUSE.

— DEODORISE THE KIDS' TRAINERS.

— TEACH MYSELF MANDARIN.

— LAG THE PIPES AND INSULATE THE LOFT.

— VACUUM THE CAR.

— CLEAN THE MOULD FROM THE GROUTING IN THE BATHROOM.

— MAKE A DRAUGHT-EXCLUDER IN THE SHAPE OF A SNAKE.

— IRON ALL THE TOWELS.

— CREATE A CARD-INDEX SYSTEM FOR MY VIDEO CASSETTES.

— ARRANGE MY CD COLLECTION BY COLOUR.

— TELEPHONE THE NEIGHBOURHOOD WATCH CO-ORDINATOR EVERY
    HOUR TO TELL HER EVERYTHING'S OK AT OUR END OF THE STREET.

— CHOOSE A FAVOURITE SPICE GIRL.

— PRACTISE CALLIGRAPHY BY WRITING OUT WAR AND PEACE LONGHAND.

— STUDY THE PAMPHLETS LEFT BY THE JEHOVAH'S WITNESSES.

TOTAL ABSTINENCE

Despite everything I have attempted to spell out about the joys of Christmas, there will still be those who have no notion of how to make the most of this very special season. These are the same people who win the lottery and blow it all on a round-the-world cruise and a Ferrari, instead of putting the money in the bank at a reasonable rate of interest and taking their holidays in Cleethorpes.

To them, I offer some tips for totally 'opting out', when there really is no other solution in sight. For example, as the festive season approaches you could begin a night-school course on transcendental meditation, yoga or the Alexander technique (whatever that may be!). As the dreadful day nears, you'll be able to move to a higher plane, and float through the festivities unperturbed ... like those strange Natural Law people who never seem to get many votes at general elections. If you have a busy lifestyle that prevents you from spending a few nights a week with a bunch of sad hippies, then a couple of tranquilizers and a bottle of vodka will induce a similar sensation of calm, weightlessness and nirvana.

Then there are those who like to feel rather more smug and superior than the rest of us. Well, fine, and why don't you spend December flushing out your system with a diet of brown rice, salt water and grape juice? You'll need very well-maintained plumbing, and come 6 January you'll look and feel terrific ... while the rest of us mope around WeightWatchers humming 'I Am the Walrus'.

On the big day itself, it's always worth remembering that zoos remain open throughout this period – after all, the animals still have to be fed, don't they? So why not volunteer to help out with the elephant droppings, if you catch my drift. And you'll be as far away from any children as it's possible to imagine. Well, have you ever heard any child screaming on Christmas Day that it wants to be taken to the zoo? There you are.

Some of the rather better-off people I know – film stars and so on – like to boast about how far away they're going to be over Christmas. Inevitably, they mean that they'll be in China or Ecuador or Zimbabwe, where they'll put up at some five-star sham palace, and kick up a fuss when they're not served turkey with all the trimmings at 3 p.m. precisely on Christmas afternoon.

Well, let me inform you that there are other ways of truly 'getting away from it all', such as my own favourite, reindeer rustling on the ranches of Lapland or heading for Tibet to celebrate the end of the year with the Buddhist monks who create elaborate yak-butter sculptures depicting a different story or fable each year. The sculptures reach thirty feet high, and are lit with special butter lamps. Awards are given for the best butter sculptures ... after which I imagine they toast a large number of muffins and crumpets. Or let your friends know that you'll be forgoing the Christian festival in order to partake of the ancient traditions

HOLIDAY HELL

A former gas engineer spent £10,000 of his redundancy pay to take his wife and family to Tenerife for Christmas.
The dream holiday turned into a nightmare when:
● Nineteen of the family were struck down with a chronic tummy bug.
● Two children were rushed to hospital when they became seriously ill.
● Their dad broke a toe when he stubbed it on a chair in their apartment.
The horror holiday ended with a four hour delay at the airport.

Daily Star 07/01/97

of Pakistan which easily pre-date the New Testament era. Around the winter solstice, an ancient demigod returns to collect prayers and deliver them to Dezao, the supreme being. During these celebrations, women and girls are purified by taking ritual baths. The men pour water over their heads while they hold up bread. Then the men and boys are purified with water and must not sit on chairs until evening when goat's blood is sprinkled on their faces. Following this purification, a great festival begins, with singing, dancing, bonfires and feasting on goat tripe and other delicacies. I've invited Glenda Jackson to join me there next year. I do have a feeling we'll both enjoy it enormously.

POSTCARD

Having a great
christmas
without you all!
R.W.

NR SANTA

ME OF PASSENGER
Richard Wilson
NON TRANSFERABLE

RESTRICTION

OT VALID BEFORE

OT VALID AFTER

RESERVAT

FARE BAS

GOOD FOR PASSAGE

FROM   Here!

TO   Away from it all!

TAX TO

ISSUE

EQUITY AMF PAID

TOTAL   ISSUED IN CONJUNCTION WITH

For those, like my friend Alan Rickman, who prefer to go even further (afield, I mean, please don't be smutty) then there is a most unusual event which takes place in Oaxaca, Mexico, on 23 December each year. It dates back to the mid-nineteenth century, and commemorates the introduction of the radish by the Spanish colonists. Radishes in this region grow to the size of turnips, but are not the rounded shape we usually see. They are twisted and distorted by growing in the rocky soil – much to the delight of Esther Rantzen, dare I suggest! These unusual shapes are exploited, as local artisans carve them into elaborate scenes from the Bible, from history and from the Aztec legends. Cash prizes are awarded, and the evening culminates in a spectacular firework display.

For those who have little to lose by obtaining a criminal record, some fun could be had on Christmas Eve, which will result in a festive break at Her Majesty's pleasure. In this way, you can be assured that you will not even get a whiff of turkey, pudding, mince-pies or alcohol. If all else fails, you will be left with no alternative but to resort to the drastic Final Solution. This, however, comes with a health warning, as its effects could be terminal, so please take adequate precautions before embarking on this procedure. For those who are aware of the potential consequences, here – in outline – is the *modus vivendi* undertaken by a very select group:

Stop the newspapers. Administer to the television screen a smart tap with a hammer. Give the radio a hot bath. Double-lock all doors. Black out the windows. Dig a trench in the back garden, and bury the telephones. Buy a book on the joys of cultivating spring bulbs. Hire a sunbed. Turn up the central heating to full. Change into swimwear. And it will almost seem as though Christmas never happened.

Christmas must be finally over because:

Today I stopped humming the theme to 'The Great Escape.'

Even Bernard Matthews couldn't get any more meat off that bird.

The dog has stopped vomiting up cracker presents.

The barmaid has finally taken off those bauble earrings.

The local Rotary Club Santa has stepped down from the trailer and been returned to his secure unit.

Easter Eggs have gone on sale in Woolworths.

I joined a mile-long queue for returns at Marks and Spencer.

My 'Seasonally Affected Disorder' has kicked in.

The boss has recognised the photocopy on the staff notice board as my arse.

I can no longer buy advocaat for love or money.

NOW IT'S ALL OVER

Oh no it isn't. It's only just beginning, all over again!